Employment Records Handbook

D1799681

PAUL TICHER
AND
GILL TAYLOR

658.
3
TICH

DIRECTORY OF SOCIAL CHANGE

Published by:
Directory of Social Change
24 Stephenson Way
London NW1 2DP
Tel: 08450 77 77 07, fax: 020 7391 4804
E-mail: books@dsc.org.uk
Website: www.dsc.org.uk
from whom further copies and a full publications list are available.

The Directory of Social Change is a Registered Charity no. 800517

First published 2005

ISBN 1 903991 39 0

British Library Cataloguing in Publication Data
A catalogue record for this book is available from the British Library

Cover design by Tessa Pellow
Typeset by Tradespools, Frome, Somerset
Printed and bound by Antony Rowe, Chippenham, Wiltshire

Other Directory of Social Change departments in London:
Courses and Conferences 08450 77 77 07
Charity Centre 08450 77 77 07
Charityfair 020 7391 4875

Directory of Social Change Northern Office:
Federation House, Hope Street, Liverpool L1 9BW
Courses and Conferences 08450 77 77 07
Policy & Research 0151 708 0136

The authors acknowledge the assistance of Nathan Coffey from the Bates Wells & Braithwaite employment team in reviewing the legal advice provided.

CONTENTS

ABOUT THE AUTHORS

Gill Taylor MA, MCIPD, is the Director of Connections Partnership and has more than 21 years' work and consultancy experience in the voluntary sector. She is passionate about the importance of personnel skills for managers, and specialises in all aspects of personnel management. Gill has written ten personnel books for the voluntary sector.

Paul Ticher has over 25 years' experience in the voluntary sector, as an information worker, manager and board member in local and national charities. Since 1991 he has worked as an independent consultant specialising in Data Protection, information management and IT strategy. Paul is also a widely-respected researcher, trainer and author, and has written books and shorter publications on Data Protection.

Disclaimer

This book does not give a full statement of the law, in particular where the position in Wales, Scotland or Northern Ireland differs from that in England, nor does it reflect changes after 31 January 2005. It is intended for guidance only, and is not a substitute for professional advice. No responsibility for loss occasioned as a result of any person acting or refraining from acting can be accepted by the publisher or by the authors.

GLOSSARY

Certain phrases are generally used in this book with a specific meaning, often tied in with legal provisions. The main ones are given here, along with an explanation of abbreviations that have been used. In the text of the book, to indicate specifically that a word or phrase is used with a precise meaning, it may be enclosed in quotation marks.

For organisations see further information in Chapter 18. For Data Protection Act definitions see Chapter 3, except where indicated.

Acas	Previously the Advisory Conciliation and Arbitration Service.
AUP	Acceptable use policy (usually covering information technology and especially e-mail, sometimes also telephones).
Care Standards	Used in this book to refer to all activities encompassed in the Care Standards Act 2000, its associated Regulations, National Minimum Standards and inspection regime.
CRB	The Criminal Records Bureau
CSCI	The Commission for Social Care Inspection
Data controller	The body or individual that bears legal responsibility for Data Protection compliance (in the context of this book almost certain to be the employer in most cases).
Data processor	An organisation that processes personal data on behalf of a data controller.
Data subject	The individual to whom personal data relates.

Disability or 'Double tick' symbol

A green circle with two ticks inside it indicating employers who have agreed to meet five commitments regarding the recruitment, employment, retention and career development of disabled people. More details on the Job Centre Plus web site (see the Resources section on page 187).

The 'Durant' case	Durant v Financial Services Authority, [2003] EWCA Civ 1746, in which the Court of Appeal considered the precise definition of personal data.

EEA   European Economic Area: Austria, Belgium, Cyprus, the
                        Czech Republic, Denmark, Estonia, Finland, France, Ger-
                        many, Greece, Hungary, Iceland, Ireland, Italy, Latvia,
                        Liechtenstein, Lithuania, Luxembourg, Malta, the Nether-
                        lands, Norway, Poland, Portugal, Slovakia, Slovenia, Spain,
                        Sweden and the UK (this is the European Union and three
                        other countries).

Genuine Occupational Requirement
                        Permits employers to treat people differently if it is a
                        genuine requirement that a person of one sex, a particular
                        race, a particular sexual orientation, or with a particular
                        religion or belief be employed in that particular job.

HSE   The Health and Safety Executive

Lawful Business Practice Regulations
                        The Telecommunications (Lawful Business Practice) (Inter-
                        ception of Communications) Regulations 2000 (SI 2000 No.
                        2699).

List 99   The 'list of individuals who are considered unsuitable to
                        work with children', established by the Protection of
                        Children Act 1999.

OPAS   The Pensions Advisory Service

Personal data   Information about an individual which is regulated by the
                        Data Protection Act (including most personnel records, but
                        not necessarily all).

POVA   Protection of Vulnerable Adults (normally used to refer to
                        the list of people unsuitable to work in specified roles
                        because of the risk they might pose to vulnerable adults).

RIDDOR   Reporting of Injuries, Diseases and Dangerous Occurrences
                        Regulations 1995

SAP   Statutory Adoption Pay

Sensitive data   Data in specific categories, defined in the Data Protection
                        Act, which by its nature carries a greater risk if misused.

SMP   Statutory Maternity Pay

SPP   Statutory Paternity Pay

SSP   Statutory Sick Pay

Subject access   The right of an individual to see, and if they wish have a copy of, personal data about them held by a data controller (see Chapter 7).

TOIL   Time off in lieu (of overtime that has been worked but will not be paid for).

1 INTRODUCTION

Unlike many books on personnel practice, this one concentrates on the very practical question of record-keeping, both the 'what?' and the 'how?'. If you are new to personnel management, or if personnel management is just one part of a wide-ranging set of responsibilities, we hope you will find this book a useful companion to those that focus more on how to manage people. Many of these say something like 'Keep a record of your disciplinary meeting', but without going into any more detail. This book gives you, in one place, a comprehensive picture of what your employment records should look like.

The book covers:

- the main legal requirements for record-keeping in areas such as recruitment and selection, employment contracts, pay and prevention of discrimination;
- practical areas where you may need to record evidence that you have followed the correct procedures, such as probationary periods;
- tricky issues that may well arise – such as when you should disclose information about your staff to other organisations and when you should not;
- good practice, both for the employing organisation and for the well-being of staff.

You will find here recommendations and practical examples for the whole of an employee's time with an organisation, from recruitment and selection through to leaving the organisation – and beyond.

You might feel that all this paperwork causes unnecessary fuss and bureaucracy. Painful experience over many years, in many organisations, suggests otherwise. Should things start to go even a little bit wrong, you will be extremely grateful that you have top quality personnel records.

Some record-keeping is legally required. It is not worth taking the risk of falling foul of the law. Much record-keeping is about being clear over contractual and procedural issues. That's why it has to be accurate and rigorous, and why it will at some point stand you in very good stead. It saves a lot of potential trouble if everything is recorded in a way that is agreed and cannot easily be challenged by different versions of events.

Experienced personnel managers and volunteer managers may well find that much of this is second nature. However, by covering all record-keeping issues in one place, we hope that this book will enable you to carry out a quick quality-check on your organisation's record-keeping, and that it may remind you of areas you have quietly forgotten, or where the situation has changed recently.

The Data Protection Act 1998 introduced a new element into the equation: in order to promote good practice in this area the Information Commissioner has issued a Code of Practice on the keeping of employment records (see page 18). While compliance with the Code is not a legal requirement, the Code does set out an authoritative view on how the legal requirements in the Data Protection Act can be complied with. Anyone who chooses not to follow the Code may have to show how their approach complies equally well with the law.

Rather than explain the Code in isolation, this book incorporates its standards and guidance into the relevant sections. We do not explain in detail how each example or recommendation aids compliance with the Act; instead, a separate chapter summarises the Principles behind it. If you are unfamiliar with the Data Protection Act, this will put things into context.

One thing this book is not about is the actual employment procedures which your record-keeping supports, although inevitably it draws on examples of good practice. Publications and resources that can help you achieve good employment practice are listed in the Resources section on pages 183–4.

The layout of this book

The book starts with a summary, pulling together all the main recommendations into a checklist which should help you to identify any areas where you need to take action. Then there are five chapters that look at overall issues:

- the Data Protection Principles;
- how you should keep your employment records;
- the requirements of a personnel records system;
- retention periods: how long you should keep your personnel records;
- the individual's right of access to their own records.

The chapters that follow look in more detail at the stages of an employee's career with an organisation:

- recruitment and selection;
- contracts;
- induction and probation;
- holidays, sickness absence and health records;
- performance records and monitoring;
- leaving the organisation.

Separate chapters look at:

- disclosing information about your staff;
- the kind of written employment policies you may need;
- particular issues that arise with overseas workers;
- volunteer records (see also below).

The extensive appendices at the end of the book give examples of many of the forms that you are most likely to need, as well as more detail on the applicable legislation.

The book is as up-to-date as possible, in a rapidly changing world. We have tried to give examples that are detailed enough to be useful, without being so dependent on specific legislation that they rapidly become wrong or misleading. Look in the Resources section (page 181) for the best place to check on the latest position.

Legislation varies across the United Kingdom. There are small differences between England and Wales, larger differences with Scotland and Northern Ireland. However, there are very few cases where this affects good practice, and the book is written to be generally applicable. Readers in England can assume that legislation referred to in the text applies to them, unless stated otherwise. In most cases it will also apply – or equivalent legislation will apply – in Wales, Scotland and Northern Ireland. Significant variations are pointed out in the Resources section (page 181) and in Appendix A.

A note on the 'personnel department'

Many voluntary organisations are too small to have a personnel department as such. They may not even have a staff member whose sole responsibility concerns personnel issues; often these fall to the chief officer, another manager, or even a relatively junior person. Volunteers may be recruited and administered by staff completely separate from those concerned with paid staff. In some cases payroll or other personnel functions may be outsourced, or carried out by consultants or management committee members.

To avoid having to acknowledge the full range of possibilities on each occasion, this book uses the term 'personnel department' as shorthand for whoever in the organisation has responsibility for the administration of personnel records and for guiding other staff in personnel matters – or their equivalent in relation to volunteers.

A note on 'in the file'

In most cases it makes no theoretical difference whether information is held in electronic form or on paper. It is purely a matter of administrative convenience and practical arrangements. There is a discussion in Chapter 4 comparing the security and other aspects of the two options. Elsewhere, when the term 'in the file' or something similar is used, this should be taken to include both paper and electronic systems unless the context requires otherwise: for example where an original document is being kept.

A note on terminology for workers

In some contexts the terms 'employee' and 'worker' have specific legal meanings, which are discussed in Appendix B. In most cases there is little practical difference from the point of view of record-keeping, and we only use these terms in their strict legal sense when distinguishing between the two. The Information Commissioner's material uses 'workers' as a general term, and this usage has not been changed where material is directly quoted.

Where we use the word 'staff' or 'personnel' this could include employees and/or workers according to the context. Many organisations also regard volunteers as part of their staff, but it is very important to be clear about volunteers' different status. A volunteer is not just someone who works for you without pay. Legally there must be no employment relationship. This will be judged on all the facts of how you relate to the people you call 'volunteers' and the expectations you create, including the content of the records you keep. See the Resources section (page 181) for guidance on where to find more information.

Volunteer records should be treated according to the same principles, and just as carefully, as those of paid staff. In order not to introduce confusion over the legal position, volunteers are considered separately in Chapter 17.

CHECKLIST OF RECOMMENDATIONS

Throughout the book we recommend good practice as well as outlining key legal requirements. Some of the suggestions will only be relevant to particular situations, so this is not a comprehensive list. Instead, it is a list of the main things you may have to consider, and an indication of where you will find them referred to in the book.

Chapter 3

Have you allocated overall responsibility for Data Protection issues? ☐
> Who will oversee policies, train staff and deal with problems?

Chapter 4

Have you allocated responsibility for personnel records? ☐
> Who is the 'owner' of your records? Who defines what is held and how?

Are your personnel records kept confidential? ☐
> Do your staff know what access is allowed and do they enforce this?

Do people outside the personnel department hold only the minimum personnel information? ☐
> Are you sure your line managers are complying?

Does your organisation set appropriate standards of security? ☐
> Do these cover both electronic records and those held on paper?

Chapter 5

Have you set up an appropriate personnel records system? ☐
> Is each type of information held in the most appropriate way and location?

Are different types of information separated out? ☐
Can people look up one area without straying into more
confidential areas?

**Do you have reliable systems for keeping the information
up-to-date?** ☐
Is it easy for members of staff to update information about
themselves?

**Do you have efficient procedures for passing information between
the personnel department and payroll?** ☐
What about finance? Training?

Do you keep a record of non-routine file accesses and disclosures? ☐

Chapter 6

Have you established a clear and practical retention policy? ☐
Do your retention periods protect the organisation as well as
individuals?

Chapter 7

Have you set up a clear procedure for handling subject access? ☐
Are you sure you can comply within the 40-day time limit?

Have you decided whether to have an open files policy? ☐

Chapter 8

Do your recruitment materials give a fair picture of the job? ☐
Are your advert, job description, person specification, etc, accurate?

Do your application forms ask for the right information? ☐
Are they aimed at helping you to choose between applicants?

Do your application procedures maintain confidentiality? ☐

Do your interviewers know what to record and how? ☐

Do you make the right pre-employment checks, in the right way? ☐
Do you check: references, qualifications, eligibility to work, CRB?

After the decision, do records get kept or destroyed appropriately? ☐
>Do the right bits get transferred to the successful applicant's
>personnel file?

Chapter 9

Are your employment contracts up-to-date? ☐
>Do they comply with the latest legal requirements?

**Do you have good records of contract dates and changes, for
all staff?** ☐
>Can you always tell who was on exactly what contract(s) at any
>given date?

Are contracts issued and changed only according to set procedures? ☐
>Are all contracts and contract changes authorised by the right person?

Chapter 10

Do you induct new staff systematically and record this properly? ☐
>Can you prove that staff were properly inducted?

Are probationary periods clearly defined and properly managed? ☐
>Are you clear about how to dismiss someone if they are unsatisfactory?

Chapter 11

**Do you have a good system for recording both planned leave and
unplanned absence?** ☐
>Does it ensure that reasons for absence are confidential?

**Do you comply with the latest requirements on disability
discrimination?** ☐
>Do you know how to record disability information appropriately?

Chapter 12

**Do your line managers know how to conduct and record
supervisions?** ☐
>Are the records held confidentially and copied to the personnel
>department?

Do you record staff training and other development appropriately? ☐
   Can you quickly review an individual's training record?

Do you have clear and satisfactory disciplinary, grievance and appeal procedures? ☐
   Are these compliant with the latest legal requirements?

Is your time recording system fit for purpose? ☐
   Do people follow it?

Is your ethnic monitoring of staff fully justifiable? ☐
   Do you give people a genuine chance to opt out?

Chapter 13

Are you clear about which personnel information it is appropriate to disclose? ☐
   Do all your staff follow consistent guidelines?

Do you have a clear and consistent policy on giving references? ☐
   Are you clear when these are confidential?

Do you have a procedure for authorising exceptional disclosures? ☐
   Does this include times when you need to report staff for serious misconduct?

Chapter 14

Do you have a staff handbook? ☐
   Does it avoid making provision for contractual matters?

Chapter 15

Do you have a procedure for when staff leave the organisation? ☐
   Does it include a checklist of activities and a retention schedule for records?

OVERVIEW OF DATA PROTECTION

Data Protection need not be complicated. Although it imposes specific legal obligations, it is often useful to consider the requirements under three headings, and probably in this order of priority:

- preventing harm to individuals whose data you hold, or to other people;
- maintaining a good relationship with those individuals; and
- complying with specific legal requirements.

Under the heading of 'preventing harm' you must, for example, ensure that the data you hold is accurate enough for the purpose and is held securely. Poor record-keeping could lead to someone missing out on access to internal promotion, or receiving an inaccurate reference. Revealing inappropriately that an employee is receiving your support over a problem with alcoholism might lead to a lack of trust and other serious problems within their team, which could worsen the problem. 'Harm' could be anything: physical, financial, psychological, or a serious breach of privacy.

Maintaining a good relationship often ties in closely with good practice. Most voluntary organisations would want to follow good practice as a matter of course, and the best approach here is often to treat other individuals as you would want to be treated. Under this heading would come matters such as ensuring that individuals know what you do with the data you hold about them, making sure that you don't ask unnecessarily intrusive questions, and giving people a choice, where possible, over the way you use their information.

Many of the remaining legal requirements are unlikely to be relevant in relation to personnel records. However, this category would include the right of an individual to access the data you hold about them (see Chapter 5), and the need to have a compliant contract when you outsource personnel or payroll activities.

The eight Data Protection Principles

The Data Protection Act 1998 covers these key ideas in its eight Data Protection Principles. These Principles are mandatory; if you hold information about individual people you must comply with the Principles at all times, but there is usually plenty of scope for deciding how to comply. In essence, this is what the Principles say.

---

1 You must be fair to the data subject, stay within the law, and have a sound basis for collecting, holding or using information about any individual.

2 When you obtain data, you must have a specific purpose or purposes in mind, and all action that you take concerning the data must be compatible with the original purpose(s).

3 The data you hold must be adequate, relevant and not excessive in relation to your purpose(s).

4 The data you hold must be accurate and, where necessary, kept up-to-date.

5 You must not keep data longer than necessary for your purpose(s).

6 You must respect the rights of data subjects.

7 You must take appropriate technical and organisational security measures to prevent unauthorised access, loss or damage to data.

8 If you intend to transfer data abroad, you must ensure that it stays protected, or else, in most cases, obtain consent from the data subject.

Data Protection Principle 1: Fair and legal

The key to compliance with this Principle is transparency: ensuring that you do not deliberately keep the data subject in the dark, or go behind their back. In the employment context, most of what you do will be obvious to the data subject and will raise few areas of concern. However, examples of possible problems, which will be covered in detail later in the book, include the following.

- Do people applying for jobs know enough about how the information they supply is going to be used? (See Chapter 8.)
- When you hold emergency contact details do those emergency contacts know that you have information about them? (See Chapter 5.)
- Do your employees know which other organisations you routinely pass their information to (such as pensions companies or occupational health services)? (See Chapter 13.)
- If you carry out monitoring of your workforce, do they know this, and are you sure that you comply with the restrictions in the Lawful Business Practice Regulations. (See Chapter 12.)

■ Does your personnel department know when it is 'fair' to pass information about your staff to outside agencies, with or without their consent? (See Chapter 13.)

In addition to being 'transparent', you are required to meet at least one of the 'conditions' for fair processing. In most cases where employment records are concerned this is unlikely to be a problem. However, *everything* you do with the data must meet a condition. This means, for example, that even when you hold data legitimately, you must not disclose it without also meeting one of the conditions – which may be the same condition as the one under which you hold the data, but does not necessarily have to be.

The conditions are set out in Schedule 2 of the Data Protection Act 1998, and are given in the box below. (Entries in italics are summarised.)

Any use of personal data must meet at least one of these conditions.

1 The data subject has given his consent to the processing.
2 *The processing is necessary for setting up or carrying out a contract to which the data subject is a party.*
3 The processing is necessary for compliance with any legal obligation to which the data controller is subject, other than an obligation imposed by contract.
4 The processing is necessary in order to protect the vital interests of the data subject.
5 *The processing is necessary for a variety of statutory and official activities.*
6 The processing is necessary for the purposes of the data controller's legitimate interests (or those of someone to whom data is disclosed), except where it prejudices the rights and freedoms or legitimate interests of the data subject.

Most uses of data for personnel purposes are very likely to satisfy the second, third or sixth condition. If not, you may need to ask for the individual's consent. In the case of the sixth condition it is particularly important that you are sure the data subject knows what you are doing in advance, so that they can alert you to any danger of your actions causing them significant harm.

There are specific Data Protection issues to do with the holding of health information about employees, which are discussed in Chapter 11.

Data Protection Principle 2: Specified purposes

In most cases your purpose in holding employment records will be restricted to activities within the standard definition given in the Information Commissioner's *Notification Handbook* (see the Resources section on page 186). This definition includes recruitment and selection, payroll, pensions, employee administration and volunteer administration.

You only need to specify any additional purposes if these are not obviously part of routine personnel activities – for example if you pass employee details to the fundraising department so that they can contact your workforce about selling raffle tickets or buying products such as Christmas cards.

The best way to 'specify' a purpose is to tell the individual(s) concerned. You could do this as part of your induction process, or by a memo or e-mail to all affected staff, for example.

Data Protection Principle 3: Adequate, relevant and not excessive

Clearly it is in your interest to have good quality data. The implication of this Principle is that you have to be very clear about what information you need and what you do not need, in respect of each person. It is not good enough, for example, to hold details of whether each staff member has a driving licence if this is a requirement in only a proportion of your posts. Equally, you should not ask for the applicant's age on an application form unless this is relevant to the selection criteria you are using; in most cases this would amount to age discrimination, which will be outlawed in 2006.

Data Protection Principle 4: Accurate and up-to-date

When your information comes from the data subject – in this case your staff or volunteers – you can usually put the onus on them to ensure that it is accurate. But you should check periodically; people will not necessarily remember to tell you when things change. You must, of course, ensure that data they give you is entered accurately. If a member of staff doesn't get paid because you put their bank details in wrongly, your organisation may well be liable not just to put matters right but also to compensate them if, as a result, their account has run dry in the meantime.

Accuracy is perhaps more of an issue with information that you add to the records, whether it is obtained from outside your organisation or internally. Opinions may be recorded, where relevant, but you must be prepared to justify them, or at least identify the source and indicate if you have not checked the information – and remember that this information would also be subject to Principle 3, above.

Accuracy when making records of complaints and allegations of misbehaviour is discussed particularly in Chapter 12.

Data Protection Principle 5: Not held longer than necessary

In the first instance it is up to you to decide how long it is necessary to keep your records. In some cases there will be legal requirements or standard professional practice to guide you. In others, a useful rule of thumb is that if you can imagine a situation – even if it is highly unlikely – when it would matter that you did not have the information, then you should keep it. You might, for example, keep details of staff involved in particularly important projects or events in case anyone wanted to follow these up in the future. You can also keep information if you have a definite plan in mind for using it (to support references you give, for example, after people have left your organisation). If neither of these situations applies, there is likely to be a case for disposing of the information.

Different information is likely to be relevant for different lengths of time, but it is important not to come up with a system that is too complicated. In the chapter summaries, retention periods are suggested for each type of material, and there is further discussion of retention policies in Chapter 6.

Data Protection Principle 6: Data subject rights

While the Data Protection Act gives data subjects several significant rights, the one which is most likely to affect employment records is that of 'subject access'. This means that your staff and volunteers have the right to a copy of virtually all the information you hold about them in your computer and paper records. This right, and the procedures you might need for providing access, are examined in Chapter 5.

Data Protection Principle 7: Security

Your security measures have to be designed to prevent two types of problem:

- unauthorised access; and
- accidental loss or damage of data.

Security is not expected to be 100 per cent effective; it must be proportionate to the risk. The security measures you take must be technical and organisational. In other words, it is not enough just to have passwords on your computers; the staff who legitimately have access to the data must also be fully aware about who they can and cannot share it with. Some of the implications of this are discussed in Chapter 4.

Data Protection Principle 8: Transfers abroad

Your responsibilities under this Principle might fall into one of two categories. If you want to put personal data onto your web site, whether text or photographs relating to individual staff members, you should as a minimum inform them beforehand and give them the opportunity to object. Unless you can legitimately claim that putting the information on the web site is necessary, and that there is no realistic alternative, you should be prepared to accede to any reasonable request for details not to appear.

The other situation is where you might want to transfer information abroad in specific circumstances, either because staff regularly work abroad or because they need to travel. In these cases it depends on the specific circumstances and on the countries to which the transfer of data is to be made. This is discussed in Chapter 16.

When is information about personnel not covered by Data Protection?

Data Protection applies to 'personal data'. A large proportion of the information you hold about staff or volunteers may well be personal data, whether you hold it on paper or computer.

In many circumstances the following, for example, could be personal data:

- photographs;
- opinions about the data subject;
- your intentions towards the data subject;
- e-mails about the data subject;
- supervision and appraisal notes, even if these are held by the line manager, not the central personnel department;
- records from an automated entry system to the building;
- closed circuit TV tapes.

Information is not covered by Data Protection requirements, however, if it is either not 'personal' or not 'data'.

The 'personal' part of the definition means that the data must be about identifiable, living individuals. Statistical data, data about the pay scales your organisation operates, or data about posts which does not relate to specific individuals (contained in recruitment material, for example) would not be personal.

As far as voluntary organisations are concerned, 'data' is information:

- held in any automated or computer-based system (on computer or CCTV recordings, for example);
- held in a 'relevant filing system'; or
- intended to go onto computer or into a 'relevant' system.

Note that for public authorities the definition of data is widened by the Freedom of Information Act 2000, to include unstructured personal information that is held manually.

Guidance originally issued by the Information Commissioner suggested that a 'relevant filing system' would include a wide variety of paper records. This was not the view of the government at the time the Bill was being debated in parliament, and a restrictive interpretation of the definition was supported in a December 2003 decision of the Court of Appeal (the Durant case – see Glossary). The court decided that manual records must be 'of a similar level of sophistication to that provided by computerised records' – in terms of their indexation, in particular – in order to comply with the definition.

The Court also decided that information is not necessarily 'personal' just because it mentions an individual. It must be *about* them in some way.

As a result of this case, the Information Commissioner has issued revised guidance in 'The Durant Case and its impact on the interpretation of the Data Protection Act 1998' (October 2004). This gives examples of information that is not normally personal:

- *mere reference to a person's name where the name is not associated with any other personal information;*
- *incidental mention in the minutes of a business meeting of an individual's attendance at that meeting in an official capacity; or*
- *where an individual's name appears on a document or e-mail indicating only that it has been sent or copied to that particular individual, the content of that document or e-mail does not amount to personal data about the individual unless there is other information about the individual within it.'*

In relation to manual files, the Commissioner says that in order for manual files to fall within the definition of a relevant filing system:

'the content will either be so sub-divided as to allow the searcher to go straight to the correct category and retrieve the information requested without a manual search, or will be so indexed as to allow a searcher to go directly to the relevant page/s.'

Only time, and perhaps further cases, will see a firm consensus emerging. However, good practice would suggest that much personnel information should be handled as though it were personal data, even if it is borderline. In this book good practice is recommended even where it is not a legal requirement.

Job evaluation scores

There is some disagreement over whether job evaluation scores are personal data. A job evaluation exercise is about scoring the post, not the individual. The scores are normally not disclosed, in order to ensure that any appeal or disagreement focuses on the fairness of the overall outcome rather than on individual scoring decisions.

There is an argument from some Data Protection practitioners that because it is known who holds what post the individual scores for the post are personal data in relation to the post-holder. However, as the scores relate to the normal performance of the post by sometimes more than one post-holder, not the individual performance of the person in the post, it could equally be argued that an individual could not claim the scores to be personal data.

Unless there is a test case, this uncertainty will remain. Meanwhile, most personnel professionals feel that it is unhelpful if the scores have to be disclosed. You may therefore wish to hold scores on paper, ensuring that all references are to the post not the post-holder, in order to strengthen the case for the scores not being personal data.

'Sensitive data'

The Data Protection Act defines certain types of data as 'sensitive'. This is data which, by its very nature, is thought to carry a particular risk of harm to the individual. For this reason, there is an additional, more stringent, set of Conditions, one of which must be met before the data can be collected or used. These conditions are set out in Schedule 3 of the Act, with additional conditions in the Data Protection (Processing of Sensitive Personal Data) Order 2000 (SI 2000 No. 417).

Sensitive data is defined in the Act as:

'personal data consisting of information as to –
(a)   the racial or ethnic origin of the data subject,
(b)   his political opinions,
(c)   his religious beliefs or other beliefs of a similar nature,

(d) *whether he is a member of a trade union (within the meaning of the Trade Union and Labour Relations (Consolidation) Act 1992),*

(e) *his physical or mental health or condition,*

(f) *his sexual life,*

(g) *the commission or alleged commission by him of any offence, or*

(h) *any proceedings for any offence committed or alleged to have been committed by him, the disposal of such proceedings or the sentence of any court in such proceedings.'*

Other material, even things people feel sensitive about, such as their age, does not have to meet one of the special Conditions.

Rather than give here a full list of the Conditions under which 'sensitive' data may be processed, relevant Conditions are discussed at various points in the book when particular types of sensitive data are under consideration.

The data controller

Occasionally there is some difficulty in identifying the 'data controller' – the legal 'person' with responsibility for Data Protection compliance. The data controller in the context of this book can normally be taken to be the employing organisation. It is most unlikely to be an individual, and almost certainly never an employee in the personnel department.

Even in an unincorporated organisation, for day-to-day purposes the organisation can be regarded as the data controller. If enforcement or other legal action were ever taken, however, it would have to be taken against named individual trustees or managers.

Care must be taken where the legal structure is not straightforward. Where, for example, a charity has a linked trading company, but staff are employed who carry out work for both organisations, it is possible that the two organisations would be joint data controllers of the same set of personnel data. Although each would have their own legal responsibilities in such a case, it would obviously make sense for them to agree on and follow a common policy.

In the case where one or more people are employed to service the work of a consortium, the possibilities are even more complex. It could be that the single organisation legally employing the staff is the data controller; it could be that all members of the consortium are joint data controllers; or it could be that the consortium itself is the data controller. Legal advice should be sought if there is any doubt in specific cases.

Where staff are seconded from one organisation to another, there is likely to be a transfer of personnel data between the two organisations, each acting as a separate data controller in respect of the data it holds.

The Information Commissioner's Codes of Practice

The Information Commissioner has powers to issue Codes of Practice on different aspects of Data Protection compliance. Among the first of these is a Code covering employment records. This is in four parts dealing with the following.

1 Recruitment and selection.
2 Employment records.
3 Monitoring employees.
4 Information about workers' health.

The first two parts were issued under the aegis of Elizabeth France, who preceded the current Commissioner, Richard Thomas. They are lengthy and detailed. Richard Thomas has announced his intention to simplify Data Protection compliance wherever possible. In issuing the much-delayed final versions of Parts 3 and 4 – the latter only in December 2004 – he demonstrated his intention by simultaneously issuing much shorter and simpler summaries, intended to be suitable for small businesses (and therefore small voluntary organisations).

These Codes of Practice are guidance. They are not necessarily the final word on the law. Although they have been prepared carefully and with the involvement of the Commissioner's legal team, they can be overturned by the courts. Compliance with the Codes is, however, given serious weight by the courts and, should it come to legal action, anyone who was not following the Code would have to demonstrate that their approach was in fact compliant with the Act itself.

This book therefore takes the view that the Code should be complied with unless there is very good reason not to, although many of the detailed provisions of the Code are likely to be applicable only to larger organisations.

The Codes are written as a series of standards, followed by discussion on how best to meet each standard. The relevant standards are quoted in the appropriate chapters of this book, but no attempt is made to demonstrate how the line taken by the book complies specifically with each standard.

Outsourcing work to data processors

Where you outsource operations which involve access to personal data, you are likely to be employing a 'data processor'. This might, for example, be a payroll bureau.

The Data Protection Act requires that you take responsibility for their actions. In other words if the payroll bureau fails to pay salaries on time, for example, it is your job to sort things out and compensate any employees who have lost out as a result.

In particular you have to be satisfied that the data processor has appropriate security – which should be at least as good as you would have if you were employing staff to carry out the task in house. Would you require Criminal Records Bureau (CRB) checks? Would you expect staff to sign up to a confidentiality pledge? Would you keep the information under lock and key, or on a secure computer? These are the kind of measures you would therefore expect a data processor to take.

Prudent business practice would suggest that you should have a solid contract with your data processor; the Data Protection Act makes this a requirement.

Information Commissioner's benchmarks on outsourcing data processing

1 Satisfy yourself that any data processor you choose adopts appropriate security measures both in terms of the technology it uses and how it is managed.

2 Have in place a written contract with any data processor you choose that requires it to process personal information only on your instructions, and to maintain appropriate security.

3 Where the use of a data processor would involve a transfer of information about a worker to a country outside the European Economic Area, ensure that there is a proper basis for making the transfer.

Chapter summary

Data Protection is principally about:

■ preventing harm to individuals whose data you hold;
■ maintaining a good relationship with those individuals; and
■ complying with specific legal requirements.

The Act applies to virtually all information about individuals that is held electronically and to much of what is held on paper. Even where information is not strictly covered by the Data Protection Act, or is borderline, it is usually good practice to treat it carefully as though it were covered.

The Data Protection Act requires you to follow the eight Data Protection Principles. For employment records, the main implications of the Principles are:

- to have good quality data that is fit for purpose;
- to hold only data that can be justified;
- to ensure that data is only used in ways that are fair to the individual, and reasonably predictable (or that the individual is informed, where this is not the case);
- to make provision for complying with the individual's legal right of access to (and a copy of) most of the information that is held about them, both on paper and electronically.

The Information Commissioner has issued guidance on how employment records should be handled in order to comply with the Act, in a four-part Code of Practice. This book broadly follows the Code.

Any external organisation you contract with to process your personnel data is likely to be a 'data processor'. You must have a written contract with them, and take responsibility for their actions.

chapter 4

HOW YOU SHOULD KEEP PERSONNEL RECORDS

Employment records should be confidential. This does not mean that they are secret. There may be all sorts of good reasons why a wide variety of people need to know things about your staff. However, people should only be given access to the information if they have a good reason for needing it.

You should also avoid holding duplicate information as far as possible. If one copy of a document or record is updated, there is no guarantee that any others will be – or your procedures to make this happen will have to be that much more complicated. You also have less control over access if the information is in more than one place. What this all boils down to is that your main personnel records should be kept in one secure location (or two if you have some records on paper and some in electronic form).

Larger organisations

In large organisations the main location for records will obviously be the personnel or human resources department. There are in addition questions about how much also needs to be held by the finance department (mainly for payroll, but possibly also for budgeting purposes) and how much needs to be held by departmental heads, branch office managers or line managers.

A few general rules for larger organisations are worth considering.

- The personnel department is the 'owner' of all personnel files. This means that even when information is not actually held in the department it must be held according to procedures laid down by that department.
- Information is passed to other departments according to clear procedures, and only to the extent necessary. For example, the finance department need to know when someone is off sick, but they do not need to see the certificates detailing the reasons.
- Managers hold only those records or pieces of information that are relevant to their work planning, budgeting or management of the staff concerned – holiday records, absence records, total cost of the pay package, supervision or

appraisal notes, for example. Even where the manager in question is involved in recruitment, once the person is in post the recruitment documentation is transferred to the personnel department.

■ All access to personnel information, whether by the individual concerned or by outside agencies, goes through the personnel department.

Smaller organisations

In smaller organisations, where matters are often less formal, care is still needed. There is usually even less need to hold duplicate copies of data, or to pass it around between departments.

The general rules might include the following.

■ A designated person is the 'owner' of all personnel files. This might be the chief officer or their deputy, or it might be the senior administrator or a personnel and finance officer.

■ Other staff do not hold their own files on colleagues, but obtain information from or pass it to the 'owner' as necessary.

■ Information from the individual staff member is normally added to files directly by the 'owner', or a nominated deputy, without going through other staff first.

■ All access to personnel information, whether by the individual concerned or by outside agencies, goes through the 'owner' or a nominated deputy.

> **Information Commissioner's benchmarks on managing personnel data**
>
> 1 Establish a person within the organisation responsible for ensuring employment practices and procedures comply with the Act and for ensuring that they continue to do so. Put in place a mechanism for checking that procedures are followed in practice.
>
> 2 Ensure that business areas and individual line managers that process information about workers understand their own responsibility for data protection compliance and if necessary amend their working practices in the light of this.
>
> 3 Assess what personal data about workers are in existence and who is responsible for them.
>
> 4 Eliminate the collection of personal data that are irrelevant or excessive to the employment relationship. If sensitive data are collected ensure that a sensitive data condition is satisfied.

5 Ensure that workers are aware of the extent to which they can be criminally liable if they knowingly or recklessly disclose personal data outside their employer's policies and procedures. Make serious breaches of data protection rules a disciplinary offence.

6 Allocate responsibility for checking that your organisation has a valid notification in the register of data controllers that relates to the processing of personal data about workers, unless it is exempt from notification.

7 Consult trade unions or other workers' representatives, if any, or workers themselves over the development and implementation of employment practices and procedures that involve the processing of workers' data.

Confidentiality

Some personnel information must be made explicitly public. It rarely makes sense to keep the names of your staff or their job titles secret, and you may want to go further and have photographs of staff on display or publish profiles of individuals in your newsletter. There will be other categories of information that certain colleagues need to have about each other, but which is not to be made available to the public.

These disclosures should be thought through. The 'owner' of the personnel data must make it clear which information is public, which is available only to colleagues (and to which colleagues or managers), and which is confidential.

Some information which traditionally might have been made available to colleagues may not actually be appropriate to disclose. Health information, for example, is 'sensitive' under the Data Protection Act 1998. You should think twice, at least, before having an absence chart on the wall which shows the reason for absence. While staff in a friendly, supportive team may be quite happy for their colleagues to know that they are ill, or attending hospital, this is not something you can assume. The absence chart, if you have one, should therefore show the fact that they are away, so that their colleagues can plan their work, but the reason should be confidential to the personnel department and, possibly, their line manager, depending on who is responsible for return to work procedures.

Similarly with photographs of staff: while these are not 'sensitive' in Data Protection terms, you should consider your reasons for using them. If there is a business need to identify staff or produce identity badges, then you can make it a condition of employment (although you may want to give people a veto over specific images that they are unhappy with). Where there is no business requirement, it is more appropriate to display photographs or to use pictures in publicity material or annual reports only with the consent of the individuals concerned.

In order to maintain confidentiality, all personnel information not being made available should be kept locked away if on paper, or protected by passwords and/ or other security measures on computer. The bulk of the information should be held in a designated area, which will be the personnel department if there is one, or a protected area of the computer system.

Confidentiality extends up the organisation as well as down. If the personnel department is the 'owner' of personnel data, the chief officer, other members of the senior management team, trustees or management committee members have no automatic right to look through the personnel files without good reason. That is not to say that they never have a reason to do so, just that the access must be properly authorised and justified on each occasion.

Exceptional cases in which confidentiality might justifiably be deliberately broken are discussed in Chapter 13.

Storing records on paper

Paper-based personnel files should be kept so that as far as possible data on each employee is all together in one file with that person's name on it, and all the individual files should be kept together in a personnel system. This not only makes it easier for you, it also makes both subject access (see Chapter 5) and archiving (see Chapter 15) easier.

This is, admittedly, not always as straightforward as it seems. It might seem sensible at the time to keep all the training records, say, in one place, because it makes your training administration easier, rather than updating each person's file each time they go on a training course. In the long run, however, you would have difficulty retrieving the information if you ever wanted to review an individual's training history.

You may be tempted to keep other material separate too: grievance or disciplinary cases can generate an enormous amount of paperwork, for example. While the case is in progress, it is acceptable to keep it in a separate file – especially if more than one member of staff is involved. When it is concluded, however, and the time limits for any appeal or further action have expired, the relevant material detailing the outcome should be transferred to each individual's file and anything not forming part of the permanent record should be securely destroyed (see below).

Where material *must* be kept separately – in an accident book, for example – you should put a note in the individual's file referring to the material kept elsewhere. The Health and Safety Executive have produced a new style of accident book designed to be Data Protection compliant (see the Resources section on page 188).

Where line managers keep copies of information that is in the personnel department files or (although this is usually less acceptable) additional information which is not in the main files, this must be kept in the same way: in named files, held in one secure place.

It may seem excessive to lock personnel material away. Can you not trust everyone to know that they mustn't poke around in their own or other people's files? Only you can answer this question, but experience does show clearly that voluntary organisations are not immune from the occasional employee who is unconcerned about confidentiality or downright malicious. Some justify this by claiming, wrongly of course, that Data Protection automatically allows them to see everything in their own file. Most professional personnel managers would take the 'better safe than sorry' route and keep confidential material under lock and key.

Don't forget that it is not just files in the filing cabinets that might count as personal data. A card index with emergency contact numbers is just as worthy of protection. You would not want to find that one staff member had started harassing another, using a home phone number gleaned from the index box left unguarded on your desk. Staff who are happy for their colleagues to phone them at home can always give out their number if they wish.

A further refinement is to keep a record of file access by people who would not normally be authorised. This should show who accessed the file, the date, and the reason given. This acts as a deterrent to those – even perhaps quite senior in the organisation – who might be tempted to abuse their position without a good reason for looking in the files. It also provides an audit trail should there be any query about who had access to particular information when making decisions.

Storing records electronically

For many organisations, electronic record-keeping is the norm. Computerisation means, for example, that:

- you only have to enter information once, and can then use it in numerous different ways;
- computers are generally faster and more accurate at making calculations than human beings;

- information can be made available to different people, at different locations, without having to copy or transfer paper documents;
- your computer system can to some extent check data as you enter it – ensuring, for example, that dates of birth appear plausible;
- the computer can often produce statistics from your raw data with very little further input from you.

Electronic records should, of course, be just as secure and just as carefully organised as paper ones. As with paper records, an audit trail showing who has had access to data and who has made changes may be valuable should anything go wrong.

Care must also be taken to avoid a security breach through access to printouts, whether shared deliberately or disclosed inadvertently by being left lying around or languishing in the waste bin.

Many organisations' introduction to the use of computers for personnel data is a payroll system. Most accounts packages now have an optional payroll module, and the decision on whether this is worthwhile for your organisation should be taken by the finance department, finance officer, accountant or treasurer.

Access to the data in a payroll system should, naturally, be very tightly controlled, almost always by a reliable password system and often by additional protection for the computer on which the system sits, or even physical separation of the computer from the network. (The latter is not normally recommended, as it makes backing up and access to other data on the network a problem.)

Storing personnel data on a spreadsheet is another easy way into some of the benefits of electronic record-keeping. You should bear in mind, though, that a general-purpose package such as a spreadsheet may not have the facility to restrict access in the same way that a dedicated program does. In order to keep the information confidential you might have to protect the file by password, for example, or store it where those who are not authorised to see it cannot access it. Spreadsheets also have the disadvantage that, unless they are set up very carefully, it is easy to lose information by writing over it, and you are unlikely to be warned if you put in data that is clearly wrong – such as implausible ages or monthly salaries. It is often wise to use a spreadsheet solely for carrying out calculations or for presentation, and to have paper documents as the primary record.

The next step up is a package, usually built around a database, which is designed specifically for personnel functions. At the top end, these systems can have automatic links to payroll and accounts packages, and modules for a variety of functions such as holiday records, absence records and rota planning. This means, for example, that once a period of unpaid leave has been entered, this immediately updates the payroll system and the individual's record. It may even be possible for employees to submit leave requests electronically, by e-mail, and to have the leave approved by their manager in the same way.

A fully-fledged personnel system can be expensive; they are likely to be more relevant to larger organisations. It is difficult to find cheaper ones with just the basic functions that smaller organisations would require, and the cost of purchase and installation may be prohibitive.

If your organisation cannot afford, or does not need, a specialist personnel database it may be tempting to try to design one for yourself. This cannot really be recommended, especially if the task falls to an enthusiastic amateur, possibly a volunteer. While such a project may be cheap and, initially, meet the organisation's needs, it is likely to be hard to upgrade or maintain, may be difficult to integrate with other software, and can suffer from poor security and poor usability. Employing an external developer is often more expensive than might be envisaged and usually takes much longer than expected. The results are often disappointing (though not always, of course), and more money has been wasted on unsuccessful database projects than on almost any other aspect of IT. It is for reasons like these that many organisations stick with tried and tested manual systems, and why this book does not assume that your personnel records will be held electronically.

See the Resources section (pages 187–8) for contacts relating to personnel databases and database development.

Security must be a strong concern on any personnel database, and here it may be trickier than with the payroll function. Often one of the selling points of a database is that parts of it can be made more widely available. It is possible to have features that allow individual staff to view their own record and amend parts of it (such as contact details) or to initiate transactions, such as booking leave. Line managers, meanwhile, can access relevant information about the staff they manage, while senior management can pull off data and statistics instead of having to ask the personnel department to provide the information.

The difficulty lies in ensuring that those who do have access are only able to see and amend those parts of the data that they are authorised to. The database itself is likely to be accessible throughout the organisation, and even from outside if there are branch offices or people working from home. When logging on cannot be restricted to specific computers, security measures must aim to verify the true identity of people attempting to gain access – it must not be possible, for example, to view a colleague's record by logging on from their computer in their absence.

Physical security

While there are many reasons for not wanting your computers to be stolen, breach of confidentiality is one serious potential consequence. Even if it is the computer, not the data, which is the target, the hard drive in a stolen computer may contain personal data. You might want to take extra security measures, such as encrypting particularly confidential data. Meanwhile, measures to prevent theft are doubly valuable, and these can include access controls to the building and to the room where the data is held, as well as shackling computers, especially portable ones, and security monitoring. Before embarking on CCTV or other types of security monitoring, you must be aware of the restrictions on this discussed in Chapter 12.

In order to protect electronic data against accidental loss or damage you must, of course, keep back-ups according to a strict and frequent timetable. At set intervals – typically once a week – a copy should be taken off-site (and kept securely) to minimise the loss of data if your premises should be damaged by fire or made inaccessible in any way.

Access to paper files must also be controlled. Access controls to the building and the room are important here, too, and procedures for ensuring that papers which are supposed to be locked away actually do end up in a lockable filing cabinet or drawer at the end of the day. Finally, there must be an appropriate level of control over access to the keys.

The most appropriate security will depend on circumstances. There is no point in having a policy of locking the room where records are held, but not the filing cabinets, if cleaners or maintenance staff automatically have unsupervised access. On the other hand, locking the room when it is unoccupied may allow staff to leave papers out during the day instead of continually getting them out and putting them away again.

Destruction of records

The confidentiality of personnel records must be maintained right up to the time when they are no longer needed.

Where paper documents are being disposed of, they should be shredded or burnt. For small quantities this can be done in-house. A commercially available shredder would normally be adequate, but if you are going to put the shredded output into your normal waste or recycling you may prefer to use one that cuts the paper across as well as into strips.

For larger quantities of paper it may be more economical to employ an external company offering secure destruction. If you do this, you should be aware that under the Data Protection Act they will be a 'data processor', and your organisation would be responsible for any security breach. You must have a written contract, setting out your expectations and their security precautions, and it would be wise to ensure that you include provision for compensation if a security breach occurs.

Electronic records are harder to destroy definitively for two reasons:

■ pressing 'delete' does not usually remove the record, it just marks the space it occupies as being available for reuse (and even after it has been written over, forensic techniques may be able to reconstruct the deleted record);

■ it is likely that there will be copies of the information elsewhere in the system and particularly in back-ups.

The first of these is probably not a great concern in day-to-day use. Once the delete button has been pressed, the effort that would be involved in an unauthorised person retrieving the data makes it unlikely to be a serious risk. Deletion certainly does become an issue, however, when you dispose of computers or pass them on to another organisation. In this case, you *must* make sure that any personal data is comprehensively erased before the computer leaves your hands, or that you pass it on to an organisation which can guarantee to erase the data – for example as part of a recycling programme.

If you want to pass on the computer in working order you should consider obtaining one of the very cheap programs that can erase data securely by over-writing it enough times to make it unrecoverable. An alternative would be to reformat the hard disk(s), although this deprives the computer of its operating system, making it harder to reuse. If you are not concerned about the computer being usable you could remove the hard disk and damage it physically so that the data it contains is effectively out of reach.

When information is backed up, it is inevitable that some of your back-ups will contain data that is subsequently deleted from the main system. Indeed, this is one of the purposes of a back-up – that you can recover data which has been deleted by mistake. What you should not do is keep back-up information indefinitely. If you need to retain material for any length of time after you have finished actively using it, it should be removed from the system and transferred to a specific archive. This not only makes the difference between live and archive data clear, it also frees up storage space on your system.

Assuming that you do a full back-up every week, or every month, and incremental back-ups in between, there is no need to keep back-ups any earlier than your most recent full back-up. If you are backing up to reusable media (such as tape), old back-ups will automatically be over-written. Where your quantity of data is small enough to be backed up to CDs or DVDs of the type which cannot be reused, you should destroy these when they are no longer needed, before disposing of them.

A security culture

Above all, staff with access to confidential data must at all times consider security issues; this should become a habit of mind. It is often said – and probably truly – that the biggest security risk is 'social engineering' where someone on your staff is tricked into revealing a password or a piece of information which is either valuable in itself or which allows the malefactor to gain access later.

Staff must be wary of disclosing even apparently innocuous information unless they are absolutely sure that they know who they are disclosing it to and that that person is authorised to have it. Temporary staff and new staff who have not built up their wariness must either be very well inducted or else protected by having more restricted access to confidential data.

Openness is good in principle. In an organisation with a strong security culture, however, this openness is not allowed to extend to gossip, well-intentioned or not, that reveals confidential information about colleagues without their approval, especially in ways that could be detrimental.

Information Commissioner's benchmarks on security

1 Apply security standards that take account of the risks of unauthorised access to, accidental loss or destruction of, or damage to, employment records.

2 Institute a system of secure cabinets, access controls and passwords to ensure that staff can only gain access to employment records where they have a legitimate business need to do so.

3 Use the audit trail capabilities of automated systems to track who accesses and amends personal data.

4 Take steps to ensure the reliability of staff that have access to workers' records. Remember this is not just a matter of carrying out background checks. It also involves training and ensuring that workers understand their responsibilities for confidential or sensitive information. Place confidentiality clauses in their contracts of employment.

5　Ensure that if employment records are taken off-site, e.g. on laptop computers, this is controlled. Make sure only the necessary information is taken and there are security rules for staff to follow.

6　Take account of the risks of transmitting confidential worker information by fax or e-mail. Only transmit such information between locations if a secure network or comparable arrangements are in place. In the case of e-mail deploy some technical means of ensuring security, such as encryption.

Chapter summary

Employment records should be confidential. Your main personnel records should be kept in one secure location (or two if you have some records on paper and some in electronic form). Only if strictly necessary should information be kept elsewhere – by line managers or the finance department, for example.

There should be a clear 'owner' of personnel records, who should manage the conditions under which other people hold or have access to them.

Security measures will vary according to whether information is held on paper or electronically. The most important aspect of any security system is that staff must understand what they are supposed to do, and not do, and must actually follow the procedures laid down.

chapter 5

YOUR PERSONNEL RECORDS SYSTEM

When setting up or reviewing a personnel records system, you must be clear about:

- what information you need in order to comply with legal requirements;
- what information you need in order to manage your personnel effectively;
- how you will maintain the necessary level of accuracy;
- how you will avoid keeping information that is not relevant, or has outlived its usefulness;
- how the data will be stored, whether electronically or on paper;
- who will have access to which parts of the data;
- how access will be restricted to those who are authorised.

> **Information Commissioner's benchmarks on collecting and keeping employment records**
>
> 1 Ensure that newly appointed workers are aware of the nature and source of any information kept about them, how it will be used and who it will be disclosed to.
>
> 2 Inform new workers and remind existing workers about their rights under the Act, including their right of access to the information kept about them.
>
> 3 Ensure that there is a clear and foreseeable need for any information collected about workers and that the information collected actually meets that need.
>
> 4 Provide each worker with a copy of information that may be subject to change, e.g. personal details such as home address, annually or allow workers to view this on-line. Ask workers to check their records for accuracy and ensure any necessary amendments are made to bring records up-to-date.
>
> 5 Incorporate accuracy, consistency and validity checks into systems.

The chapters that follow look at specific types of information in more detail, while this chapter takes an overview. The information might be kept entirely on paper, but it is likely that at least some of the material will be held electronically. The principles will be the same in either case, and it is always useful to be clear about which category a document or piece of information falls into, since this gives a good indication of its retention period and possibly its level of confidentiality.

One of the key times at which you will collect or generate information about your staff is when they start work with you. The amount of information that you will already have obtained during the recruitment process should, as we shall see, be relatively restricted, and therefore relatively little will carry through to the personnel files.

In many cases it is helpful to divide the personnel file into separate categories which are actually kept in physically separate sections within the one file, if on paper, or at least in logically separate sections, often with different access authorisation, if held electronically. This then makes it easy to refer to someone's training record, for example, without inadvertently stumbling across more confidential parts of the file.

Contractual material

This would include:

- the original application form, references and the letter of appointment, as discussed in Chapter 8;
- the 'written statement' and any other documents setting out your contract terms for an employee, including any particular terms and conditions issued to that particular person (these are discussed in Chapter 9);
- any policies or agreements that are specifically part of the contract;
- any signed confidentiality statements or acknowledgements that particular policies have been received, read and understood.

All these documents are relevant to your contract with an employee. If someone breaks their contract, you need to be able to prove what they have done in order to take any kind of remedial or disciplinary action.

If you change anything – your standard terms and conditions, for example – you cannot just retrospectively apply these to existing employees; you must go through the correct consultation and amendment procedure. This can (and often does) result in different staff being on different contracts, and it is important to know exactly where each individual stands. You must therefore keep track of changes made to each employee's contract and when these were made. If the same person does different types of work for you under different contracts, you must be sure to record their patterns of work and the different terms that apply to each period of employment or type of employment.

A signed confidentiality pledge would spell out the employee's recognition of their responsibility for confidentiality, and possibly other Data Protection matters, in relation to information about other people – clients, service users, donors, members, and so on – that they handle in the course of their job.

Signed references to other policy documents could include, for example, a drugs and alcohol policy if the nature of your work means that you have to take such precautions.

The contractual section of the file will be largely generated when someone is taken on, but can be added to from time to time during the person's employment. Material should only be removed if it has clearly been superseded by subsequent events.

It is generally recommended that the job description and person specification should not be part of the contract. A copy should nevertheless be kept on the individual post-holder's file as well as any copy held in a set of all job descriptions by the personnel department.

Even if they are not contractual, a job description or person specification should be changed only through a clear, fair process, and you must document changes properly. Where there is more than one individual carrying out a role, the job description and person specification must never be changed unilaterally by one person and their manager. You must consider the whole group of people in that role to see if the work has changed for all of them, or if it really is just one post that has changed.

Basic contact and other material

For all personnel you will need a set of standard information, probably including:

- their full name;
- their date of birth (for identification purposes);
- their home address – it is worth asking for this again, even if it is on the application form, since your new employee may, after all, have moved in order to take up the job;
- a phone number for contacting them in an emergency (for example to tell them not to come in to work if the office floods) but you can only insist on having a number if your contract specifies that they must be contactable out of hours, otherwise their own time is their own if they so choose;
- details of someone who can be contacted in an emergency (see below);
- a photograph – if there is any need to keep photographic identification of your staff (e.g. on badges) it may be reasonable to keep a copy on their file;

- a summary of other key data, such as post held, start date, current pay point and anything else that you may want to refer to quickly, without having to search through the more detailed parts of the file.

It is normally better to ask for an emergency contact, rather than next-of-kin. Next-of-kin is an official description, and may refer to someone with whom they are not particularly close, or who is not readily accessible. The emergency contact should be made aware that you have been given their details. This is partly so that they are less shocked if you do ever have to contact them; partly it is because they may be a data subject – with Data Protection rights – especially if you hold their details on computer. The best solution is usually to make sure your member of staff knows that they must tell their chosen person that they have been nominated as emergency contact.

Payroll and other financial records

Most of the necessary record-keeping for payroll, tax, National Insurance, Statutory Sick Pay (SSP) and Statutory Maternity Pay (SMP) and other similar provisions should follow the forms and procedures laid down by the relevant government departments, or electronic equivalents of these forms. Records of what has been paid will form part of your organisation's accounts, and it normally makes sense for whoever is responsible for finance or payroll to hold all records relating to financial transactions with employees, both for convenience and for security. This would include:

- National Insurance number and tax details;
- bank details;
- salary scales or hourly rates, and the date and amount of any increments;
- actual amounts of pay, including any rolled up holiday payments, and deductions;
- expenses claims;
- contributions to pension or insurance schemes;
- records of loans and other financial transactions.

The amount of duplication between personnel and finance records should be kept to a minimum. Personnel should, for example, record salary increments in individual employees' files and give Finance just a list of all changes. Personnel should record absences or other variations in hours and give Finance just a list of any consequential pay adjustments to be made each week, month or whatever.

You may, of course, have a computer system which allows automatic links to be made between the personnel records and the payroll system. In this case the personnel department should normally be responsible for entering details of salary increments and absences, but as a check you may want Finance to confirm these before they go through.

Records of CRB checks and right to work checks

Records of checks that you make at the time you take someone on may have to be kept in order to show that you did the checks properly. However, these will not be part of the 'live' personnel file. Once you have made the check and satisfied yourself that all is in order, you are unlikely to make further use of the information.

The type and amount of material to retain will be discussed in Chapter 8.

This material is also likely to be highly confidential, and probably 'sensitive' under the Data Protection Act. You should therefore keep it separately from the part of the file which is accessed routinely. You may even want to keep all records of CRB checks in a completely separate section of the filing system, with additional security.

It must, of course, be possible to retrieve the material if required. Where you may be subject to Care Standards inspections this might mean keeping the material at the site where the person works, alongside their live file; in other cases security should be paramount, even if this could cause a short delay in retrieval.

Holidays, sickness absence and other time off work

By convention, 'absence' is usually taken to mean unplanned time away from work, usually for sickness, while planned time away could be called 'leave' or just 'time off'.

When someone has time away from work, for whatever reason, your records must contain:

■ details of the actual time they were away, and the specific reason;
■ the appropriate evidence to show either that leave was agreed in advance or that absence resulted from a legitimate cause.

Where your evidence includes signed documents, the original form should normally be kept in the personnel file, in order to ensure that any subsequent disagreement or dispute can be resolved quickly. Only when there is no possibility that you might need to refer back to it should such evidence be discarded. This is likely to be at least until after the end of the current year, and quite possibly longer.

Because of the potential pay and working time implications you must record dates, in particular, with scrupulous accuracy, so that they cannot be contested in future, and relevant information must be passed on to those responsible for payroll.

In addition to the authorisation for each event, it is usually helpful to keep a summary for the whole year. With holidays, for example, you need a quick tally of how much has been taken so far, and therefore how much entitlement is left, so that you know whether a new application for holiday can be approved.

In other cases you may be more interested in the pattern: a series of odd days of sick leave on Mondays and Fridays may be a coincidence, but it may be that your employee just fancies a few long weekends, and you might want to raise the issue at supervision.

Because the needs are slightly different, some organisations record their leave and absence summaries in two separate places: a simple running total for those where the total is the key issue, and a calendar system where there might be questions about the pattern. Others combine all leave and absence onto one summary record. An example of this latter option is shown in Appendix J.

Don't forget to amend your records if anything changes. If someone is ill while they are on holiday, it is quite possible that part of what was originally holiday will be converted to sickness absence, with implications for how much holiday entitlement they now have remaining.

See Chapter 11 for a more detailed discussion on leave and absence records.

You may also use time-sheets or record people's hours – for example if they work irregular hours, if they are paid by the hour, if you need to allocate their time to different projects,or if you need a record of overtime worked and time off in lieu of overtime (TOIL) taken. As well as any summaries you make, you should keep the original records, whether these are kept by the individual and signed off by their manager, or generated through some other means, such as a clocking in system. As with leave and absence records, time-sheets and other records of hours should be kept, probably for longer than you think, in order to avoid future disputes.

Induction, training, supervision and appraisal records

This section of the personnel file may be kept by the staff member's line manager rather than by the personnel department, especially if the staff member is based away from the head office. While this is common practice, it may not be ideal. The personnel department might not receive advance warning of any emerging problem, and would have no way of checking that there is a basic level of consistency between the way different managers keep their records – or even whether they are carrying out the supervisions when they are supposed to.

For all these reasons, it is better practice for the personnel department to maintain the full, official record, but to allow line managers to keep a copy of the *current* records if this makes operational sense. Records of induction, training, supervision and appraisal should therefore be sent as a matter of course to the personnel department, with copies held elsewhere if appropriate. The line managers' records should be checked occasionally to make sure that they have accurate copies of the material they are entitled to keep and are securely destroying material once they no longer need it.

See Chapters 10 and 12 for a discussion of the contents of these records.

Records of disciplinary action or grievances

If you take disciplinary action against an employee you must, of course, keep records in their file. Chapter 12 looks at the kind of records to keep during a disciplinary process, a grievance process and any appeal process. Here we look at what needs to end up in the file when the matter is concluded.

All you really need to keep in the individual file after a disciplinary matter is a record of the allegation, a record of the final outcome and a copy of any communication with the employee over this, such as a letter issuing a warning. The letter should state clearly the outcome, any sanction that is being imposed, and the length that any warning will apply. The letter should also be clear whether, at the end of that period, the warning will be *removed* from the file, or will merely *expire* (and not be taken into further account) but be kept on the record. You must obviously follow through and remove a warning at the appropriate time if you say you will. Most employers would want a warning to stay on file, in case a pattern of behaviour develops and possibly for consideration when writing a reference. If an expired warning stays on the record you may want to mark it clearly to show that it has expired.

You should only keep any additional material, such as statements given during the investigation or notes of the panel proceedings, if there is a clear reason for possibly needing to refer back to them in the future. Provided you keep a clear statement of the nature of the misconduct or breach of procedures, the detail may well be superfluous and could be disposed of – once all possibilities for internal appeal or for an Employment Tribunal case have passed, of course.

Because disciplinary matters are likely to contain at least some confidential elements, there should be a separate section for these within your records, to avoid people seeing material inadvertently if it is not relevant. If you decide to keep more than the minimum, you should again bear confidentiality in mind and consider keeping detailed records of disciplinary matters separately altogether, not in individuals' files.

Grievances should be treated similarly – a summary of the grievance and the outcome in a confidential part of the individual file, any additional details kept securely elsewhere.

If you have to report on disciplinary matters, or if your senior management team reviews grievances in order to learn from them, this should be done anonymously if at all possible. The nature of the problem, and possibly the outcome, should be described without identifying any individuals unnecessarily.

Records of file access

You may want to keep a record of who has had access to the file and for what purpose, other than routine activities within the personnel department. This could include the following.

- Access by the individual, either under an informal arrangement or a formal Data Protection subject access request.
- Access by senior staff who would not normally see the file, for example if they are investigating concerns about the individual's performance.
- Access to all or part of the information by external bodies, official (such as the police) or commercial (such as a bank, in connection with a mortgage application), for any reason.

Miscellaneous material

Your personnel file may also have a section for additional miscellaneous material, such as the following.

- Consents to other uses of data. If staff have the option of their details being used, or not, by other people or for non-essential purposes, it may be convenient to collect all of their preferences on one form.
- Evidence of driving licences, motor insurance and other required documents. You should only collect information that you have a genuine need for. It may be sufficient just to record that you have seen the driving licence or motor insurance policy (and its expiry date), for example, rather than keeping a copy. (You may also need to see the licence again at reasonable intervals, and the insurance when it is renewed, rather than rely on the individual to inform you of any developments.)
- Equal opportunities monitoring data. Even though you may have monitored the recruitment and selection process, it is better practice to ask a new member of staff to confirm the details or supply them again (or not, if they exercise their right not to).
- Correspondence with the employee or records of matters which don't fall into any other category.

Keeping your records up-to-date

All the information you hold about staff must be fit for purpose. This means that in most cases it must be scrupulously accurate and up-to-date. Obviously this is easier to manage in relation to material that you add from time to time, such as holiday records or changes in salary. Other information, such as an employee's home address or their emergency contact number, may change without you knowing it and they may forget to tell you.

Where you have to rely on the staff member to keep you up-to-date you should make it as easy as possible for them to do this. One way is by allowing staff open access to their own files, so that they can check from time to time if they wish (but see Chapter 5 for the limits of 'open access'). It may be worth your while providing this access electronically. If everyone is connected to your network, and especially if you have an intranet, it is technically possible to allow people to log into their own personnel files and make changes. Obviously they are not allowed to change their salary or anything like that, but their access need not be restricted to their personal details. There is no reason why they should not be able to send in leave requests or absence notifications electronically, for example.

Whatever facilities you provide for people to take the initiative, you still can't rely on them to remember everything. It is therefore good practice to send everyone a copy of the basic details you hold (or prompt them to check their details on line) once a year, or at some other suitable interval, and ask them to confirm that it is correct.

It is also good practice to tidy files annually and remove anything no longer required, to avoid an accumulation of miscellaneous material whose relevance has passed.

Chapter summary

You should divide your personnel files into sections, whether held on paper or electronically, so that you can find material easily and, more importantly, protect the confidentiality of material to which access is restricted while allowing normal access to other material.

Subsequent chapters examine most categories of information in more detail.

Document	Main requirements	Retention period	File location
Contractual material	See Chapter 9		On personnel file
Contact and other details	Must be up-to-date	While employed	On personnel file
Payroll and other financial records	Accuracy	Until 6 years after employment ends	In payroll/accounts system
Records of CRB and other checks	Legal compliance	See Chapter 8	Normally held separately in personnel department
Holidays, leave and sickness absence records	See Chapter 11		On personnel file
Induction, training, supervision and appraisal records	Agreed with individual	Until 6 years after employment ends	On personnel file
Records of disciplinary action, grievances and appeals	See Chapter 12		
Records of file access	Honest and complete	While file exists	On personnel file
Miscellaneous material	Must be relevant	While relevant	On personnel file

chapter 6

RETENTION PERIODS

In the summaries at the end of each chapter where specific types of record are discussed, a retention period is suggested. Some of these retention periods may appear unnecessarily long – far longer than the record is of any direct use to you. How does this square with the Data Protection Act 1998 requirement not to keep data for longer than 'necessary'?

There are four main considerations in relation to retention periods.

- A retention period may be laid down by law, or in legal regulations.
- You may want to have information so that you can call on it in the event of a legal case.
- The information may be needed to deal with disagreements between you and the employee, short of legal action.
- If none of the above applies, there will be practical considerations.

Specific legal rules make your decision very easy. For example, Part 2 of the P45 must be kept for at least three years after the end of the current tax year; this could be almost four years after the person has left. Most accident records have to be kept for three years, but some records relating to industrial diseases have to be kept for 40 or 50 years. For organisations subject to Care Standards the Regulations set out many specific retention periods for a wide range of information.

Claims by employees to an employment tribunal or the civil court about their employment are rare, but they can and do happen. You are at a serious disadvantage if you cannot substantiate your case; it is therefore 'necessary' to hold the information while there is any possibility that you might be required to produce it.

Legal cases usually have a clear time limit. The majority of employment claims must be presented to a tribunal within three months of the person's dismissal or of the action claimed by the employee. However, some claims have a longer time limit. For example, a claim for a statutory redundancy payment may be made for up to six months (and this can be extended for a further six months if it is just and equitable to do so). A claim under the Equal Pay Act 1970 can also be made for up to six months. Claims to the civil courts and for tort and breach of contract can be delayed considerably longer: they can be made at any time up to six years after the event.

There is also a discretion to extend the time limit for most claims. Tribunals have the right to extend the time limit if it was not reasonably practicable for the employee to present the complaint within the normal three-month period. 'Practicable' depends on whether it was possible to do so. Ignorance of the three-month time limit is not enough, but ignorance of the right to claim unfair dismissal might be. For example, in the 2004 case of Marks & Spencer v Williams Ryan (UKEAT/0145/04), the claim was allowed to proceed even though it was two weeks past the three-month deadline. Following a brief conversation with a Citizen's Advice Bureau the claimant believed wrongly that she had to wait for the outcome of an appeal hearing before she could submit an unfair dismissal claim to the Employment Tribunal.

Changes made under the Employment Act 2002 (Dispute Resolution) Regulations 2004 (SI 2004 No. 752) prevent an employee bringing many complaints to a tribunal unless they have first tried to use the employer's internal grievance procedure. The time limits are extended to allow for this, in most cases from three months to six.

Tribunals also have a wider discretion to extend time limits in discrimination cases; the test is whether it is just and equitable. Additionally where there is an act or a series of related acts, if the claim in relation to the last act is in time, the tribunal can also treat the earlier acts as within time. This could, and often does, lead to a claim extending back a considerable period, even many years.

The Court of Appeal, in Robertson v Bexley Community Centre 2003 (IRLR 434), has suggested that extensions of time should be the exception rather than the rule. However, it remains to be seen whether this will lead to tribunals being less willing to extend time limits. In the meanwhile, the wisest course of action is to retain documents and other information until the possibility of a claim for which they might be relevant is minimal.

Disagreements that do not reach the legal stage are much more common; they can be time-consuming to sort out, and possibly expensive: if there is sufficient doubt about an issue, you might end up paying under a negotiated settlement. Problems can emerge long after the event – for example if a group of workers allege that they have not all been given the same deal for working over the Christmas period, several years in a row. If cases such as these cannot be resolved amicably they might end up as claims of discrimination, unfair treatment, or breach of contract. The legal time limits would then apply.

It can be hard to predict what issues will lead to trouble. Retention periods should therefore err on the side of caution where there is any possibility that the records might relate to the way you have treated an individual, or to the financial relationship between you, in its widest sense.

Legal retention limits frequently fall into one of four categories:

- short periods of three to six months;
- periods of three years, or three years after the end of the current financial year;
- periods of six or seven years;
- much longer periods: up to 40 or 50 years, or until the person concerned is well beyond retirement age, or even indefinitely.

It is not very practical to have a large number of different retention periods for material in files that are not accessed very often or may even – in the case of ex-employees – be effectively closed. You do not want to have to revisit the files every few months or even every year to carry out a further little bit of pruning. In the nature of things, even if you did set out to do this it is the kind of task which could easily be overlooked or overtaken by higher priorities. If, therefore, you have material which does not fall neatly into one of these time periods it is normally safe to keep it for longer, until the next cut-off point, provided you are sure that the risk to the individual is minimal.

When you have material for which no specific guidance is available, a good rule of thumb is to ask yourself, 'Can I imagine a situation when I would be asked for this information, and it would matter that I didn't have it?' If the answer is 'yes', however unlikely the possibility, you have a good reason to keep it. To make your life as straightforward as possible, you should try to set time limits that fit into one of the 'standard' limits outlined above.

Having set these limits, you can then plan your review schedule, weeding and archiving. Live files need fairly frequent attention. Because you could be continually adding material, some of which may have a short retention period, you should review these at least every year.

Once you close a file, you should remove any short-period material after six months – or even earlier if you are sure that there are no loose ends to tie up. You should then review the file at four years and seven years, after which any remaining material can probably be archived. If you feel that there is likely to be very little four-year material in the file, and that the risk is small, you could leave out the four-year review and just carry out a single review-and-archive after seven years.

It is not possible to give a comprehensive list of retention periods for all types of material you might hold, but the table below shows some broad categories; further suggestions are given in chapter summaries elsewhere in this book. You may also be interested to see the guidance for public authorities on the National Archives web site (see the Resources section on page 190).

Type of material	Minimum retention period	Reason
Most recruitment and selection material	6 months after the decision	Time limit for claim of discrimination
Checks (such as references) made before taking someone on and any required copies of documents	6 years after contract ends (and sometimes longer where Care Standards apply)	Evidence that checks were made
Material forming part of an employment contract	6 years after contract ends (or after that provision is superseded)	Time limit for legal claim
Specified information relating to people working in a children's home	15 years after the person has left	Statutory: Children's Home Regulations
Information relating to people working under Care Standards Regulations	Varying periods	Statutory: *Consult regulations relevant to your activities* (see CSCI web site)
Accounting records	3 years in most voluntary organisations, but 6 years for public limited companies	Statutory: Companies Act
Material related to income tax and National Insurance	3 years after the end of the tax year they relate to	Statutory: Income Tax Regulations
Pay records and relevant supporting documents	6 years	Time limit for legal claim of under-payment or unlawful deductions
Leave and absence records	6 years	May be relevant to claims of under-payment, unlawful deductions or breach of contract
Pension-related records	Money purchase: 6 years Final salary: until age 72	*Consult pension provider*
Accident books and accident records	3 years after date of last entry	Statutory: RIDDOR
Medical records relating to specific hazards such as lead and asbestos	40 years (more for ionising radiation)	Statutory: various regulations
Evidence relating to SSP, SMP, SAP and SPP	3 years after the end of the tax year they relate to	Statutory: SSP/SMP Regulations
Performance records (such as training or appraisal)	6 years after employment ends	Time limit for legal claim
Disciplinary records	6 years after employment ends	Time limit for legal claim
Material related to incidents concerning child protection or protection of vulnerable adults	*Consult regulations*	Statutory: *Consult regulations relevant to your activities*
Material that is constantly updated, such as an employee's home address	Out-of-date material should, in principle, never be in the file	Data Protection Principles
Incidental correspondence with staff members	One year after the matter is closed	Data Protection Principles

Note that these periods are the minimum. You may keep records longer if you are given professional advice to do so or have any other good reason. For example, 'accounting records' in most voluntary organisations have to be kept for three years, while records of pay have to be kept for six years. If the easiest way for you to keep a record of all the payments you have made to your staff is as part of your accounts, this would suggest that it might make sense to keep the relevant parts of your accounting records for the full six years.

The material you keep after someone has left must still be relatively accessible. You can, of course, move it out of the way if you think you are unlikely to need it, but you must be able to retrieve the information for consultation if necessary. You are also likely to be required to provide access to the information if your ex-employee makes a request under the Data Protection Act (see next Chapter).

Chapter summary

Records must not be kept longer than 'necessary'. However, there are sound legal reasons for retaining much of the material in personnel records for at least six years (and for six years after the person has left).

Disputes can and do arise; they will be much more time-consuming to resolve, and the organisation will be at greater risk, if the relevant records are not available.

Some material must be kept for longer than six years.

Your retention schedule should be practical and manageable, not over-elaborate. Having established it, you should set up a review process to ensure that files are weeded at the correct times. Files for current employees should normally be checked and weeded annually; the main review of closed files for ex-employees should be six to seven years after they have left.

chapter 7

THE INDIVIDUAL'S RIGHT OF ACCESS TO THEIR OWN RECORDS

The right of 'subject access' is one of the most important in the Data Protection Act 1998. It is the data subject's main way of checking that you are complying with the Principles, that you are not keeping individuals in the dark about how you use their data, and that the data you hold is accurate and appropriate. Most organisations receive very few subject access requests, but it is essential to make provision for complying with any that you do receive.

Alongside this, you may already have an 'open files' policy which allows staff to have controlled access to their own files. This can be valuable, but is not the same thing as subject access. The differences are discussed below.

Another variant is a system where staff take on part of the responsibility for maintaining their own records – for example by being given access to their own data on the computer system. This was also discussed in Chapter 5.

Open files and subject access

For many years, personnel professionals have been moving towards greater openness with their employees, and many organisations already have an open files policy, allowing staff to see what is in their own record, under supervision, at any reasonable time.

An open files policy is highly compatible with Data Protection subject access, but they are not the same thing. For example:

- the open files policy may allow access only to a restricted set of data – such as information held in specific, active personnel records;
- the policy may make available types of information which are not personal data, and therefore not covered by subject access;

- people who would not be eligible for the open files policy – such as unsuccessful job applicants and ex-employees – have the right to make a Data Protection subject access request.

In many cases, informal access through an open files policy will give employees the information or reassurance they are looking for, and will avoid the need for a formal subject access request. If you have an open files policy you are therefore likely to receive far fewer subject access requests. In many organisations they are very rare indeed.

An open files policy does not, however, allow you to ignore your Data Protection responsibilities. However you allow access, you must supervise the process to ensure that the employee doesn't tamper with the file. (Most won't want to, of course, but you must protect yourself against the minority who might.) You must also check through the file before you grant access, even informally, to ensure that you are not allowing the employee to see information about other people or from other people that should be kept confidential. Normally, any information that is exempt from subject access (see below) should not be divulged under an open files policy, and this should be explained to the employee.

Your open files policy, if you decide to have one, should therefore explain:

- what information about themselves you automatically allow staff to see;
- what types of information are likely to be withheld;
- whether you will provide a copy of any information if they want it;
- what the procedure is for requesting access, including any restrictions on repeat applications;
- what additional rights the individual has if they choose to make use of the Data Protection subject access procedures.

Information Commissioner's benchmarks on workers' access to information about themselves

1 Establish a system that enables your organisation to recognise a subject access request and to locate all the information about a worker in order to be able to respond promptly and in any case within 40 calendar days of receiving a subject access request.

2 Check the identity of anyone making a subject access request to ensure information is only given to the person entitled to it.

3   Provide the worker with a hard copy of the information kept, making clear any codes used and the sources of the information.

4   Make a judgement as to what information it is reasonable to withhold concerning the identities of third parties, using the guidelines given later in this Code.

5   Inform managers and other relevant people in the organisation of the nature of information relating to them that will be released to individuals who make subject access requests.

6   Ensure that on request, promptly and in any event within 40 calendar days, workers are provided with a statement of how any automated decision-making process, to which they are subject, is used, and how it works.

7   When purchasing a computerised system ensure that the system enables you to retrieve all the information relating to an individual worker without difficulty. Ensure that the supplier of a system that you will use to take automated decisions about workers provides the information needed to enable you to respond fully to requests for information about how the system works.

Data Protection subject access

The basic provision under the Data Protection Act is that a data subject is entitled to have a copy, in permanent form, of all the personal data about them that was held by the data controller at the time a subject access application was made.

There are various exclusions, discussed in the following section, but you must start by being clear about what is personal data and what is not. Whereas in day-to-day activities you may very well decide to treat all information carefully, whether or not it is technically personal data, you have to be much more precise when it comes to subject access.

It is worth making an effort to locate all the data that might be relevant, even if you then decide that some of it is not personal data. It doesn't matter where or how the information is held; if it is personal data, then it must be included. However, if the information does not fall within the definition of personal data (discussed in Chapter 3) then you do not have to provide access.

Unless you are really sure that there is no possibility of any information being held outside the main personnel record, you should do a trawl in order to be sure that you have not missed anything. It is worth considering some likely possibilities. These take account of the 'Durant' case ruling (see Glossary and page 15).

- The data subject's line manager might have a separate file on each member of their team, containing, say, absence records and training records. These files probably would be personal data.

- The chief officer's manual file labelled 'Confidential personnel matters' – perhaps surprisingly – might not be personal data, even if there were sub-sections within it for specific staff members, based on the argument that you would not know enough in advance about the content of the file for it to count as 'data'.

- The payroll information and records of salary payments held in the finance system almost certainly would be personal data, whether on computer or on paper.

- Salary data held by Fundraising in connection with funding bids might be personal data, especially if it is held electronically.

- Recordings from CCTV or entry control systems would probably be personal data.

- E-mails about the data subject would probably be personal data. Those sent to or by the data subject might be, but this area has been the subject of some discussion (see box below).

If the information held elsewhere is an exact duplicate of that held by the personnel department, then you do not need to provide both copies, but you must be certain that it is genuinely a duplicate. Discrepancies between different data sets may be exactly what the data subject is looking for.

You must not edit the record, however embarrassing it is, between receiving the request and providing access. The only changes you are allowed to make are those which would have happened at that time anyway – payroll processing, for example, or updating absence records.

Do I really have to show e-mails in responding to a subject access request? Our security archives go back over a year!

In principle, e-mails may very well be personal data if they are about a specific individual. Much vital information is now recorded in e-mails – and often nowhere else. In a subject access request, that may be the very data that the data subject is looking for. If you do not have the facility to search your archives or restore information easily, you may want to think about this.

You cannot use the excuse that finding the information is difficult in order not to give access to the data. However, the 'Durant' case made it clear that it is not sufficient merely for the individual's name to appear, whether as the sender, the recipient or in the body of the message, for the e-mail to be 'personal'. (It is certainly data, as it is held on computer.) Under a subject access request you

---

would not have to provide copies of all the business e-mails an individual had sent or received. You probably *would* have to provide any e-mails between other staff where the individual was discussed, or e-mails relating to the individual – to do with their holiday arrangements, for example.

The Information Commissioner has also published guidance on subject access to e-mails on the 'individual rights' section of their web site (although this has not been updated following the 'Durant' case). This suggests, among other things, that e-mail records might not have to be searched unless the data subject gives enough information to narrow the search down, but that a deleted e-mail would still have to be produced if it could be recovered reasonably easily from a backup.

What information can be withheld from subject access?

Subject access only applies to personal data. Your first task, therefore, is to establish what personal data you hold about the person making the access request. There are then two main types of personal data which can be withheld from subject access, although only in limited circumstances. These are:

- third party information; and
- various categories of information that is in the process of being used as the basis of decisions or actions.

'Third party' information means that either the data is about someone else (that is, not the data subject or anyone acting for the data controller), or someone else is the source of the data.

Staff, volunteers or committee members do not count as third parties where they are acting on behalf of the data controller. So, a line manager making comments about someone's work performance is not a third party; they are an agent of the data controller. However, a staff member making a complaint about a colleague is acting in their own personal capacity. In such a case they would almost certainly be a third party, as the source of the complaint, and any other colleague mentioned in the report of the complaint would also be a third party.

The issue only arises where the third party is identifiable by the data subject. Therefore, third party information where the identity will not be known, or where the identity can easily be disguised without detracting from the value of the information to the data subject, would automatically have to be provided (unless subject to another exemption).

The procedure for deciding whether or not third party material can legitimately be excluded often becomes complicated. Where the repercussions from getting it wrong could be severe, you should consider taking legal advice. Often a subject access request is made in the course of a dispute or when the data subject is already disaffected. You do not want to make a bad situation worse by failing to comply properly with the subject access request or by disclosing information that should properly have been withheld.

In general, third party material should be withheld unless:

■ the third party has given their consent to disclosure; or
■ it is reasonable to disclose without their consent.

Chart A illustrates the general process for deciding on third party material. First you have to identify whether there is any third party material in the file, then you have to decide whether it is necessary to seek consent from one or more third parties. In many cases the third party information will be relatively trivial and already known to the data subject. For example, if your employee has provided you with details of an emergency contact person, it would be perfectly reasonable to leave that information in the file for the data subject to see, without even asking for the person's consent. It is obvious that you would not be breaking any confidentiality. In other cases it might be safe to assume that you do have a duty of confidentiality. If there is a letter in the file between two departments which mentions another colleague's salary level, you might decide to blank out that information without further ado (while still showing the rest of the letter).

If it is not clear whether the information should or should not be disclosed, you will normally have to contact the third party to seek their consent. If they are happy for the information to be shown, then you must do so. Where they are not happy, a duty of confidentiality to the third party may exist. Often it will be a matter of balancing the data subject's legitimate interest in knowing what is in their files against the third party's legitimate interest in confidentiality. You could, conceivably, decide in favour of the data subject because you feel that the third party has withheld consent unreasonably. This course of action does, however, carry risks of breach of confidence, and should not be taken without legal advice. Where you cannot make contact with the third party (or have a significant reason for not wishing to), you still have to take their interests into account and make a decision as to whether it is reasonable on balance to show the information.

If there is third party material which you should withhold you must then consider whether it can be edited, or 'redacted', to remove the third party identifying details while still allowing the data subject to see the content of the information.

Chart A: Subject access to 'third party' material

NB: This relates only to access by the data subject to their own records; disclosure to other people is a completely different issue.

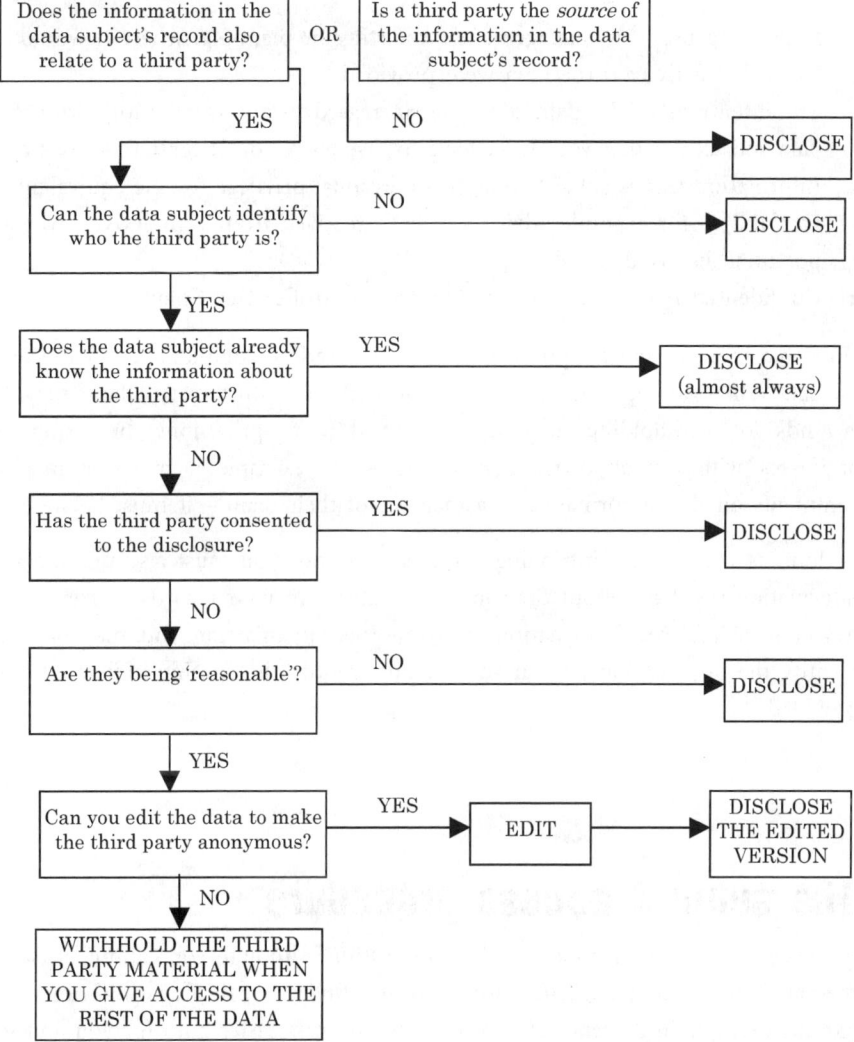

In some cases it may be possible to remove the details by merely blanking them out or providing a print-out that omits them; in others it may be more appropriate to retype the material without the identifying details.

A common instance where third party questions arise is the case of references. See Chapter 8 (incoming references) and 13 (outgoing references) for a further discussion.

Other categories of data that may be withheld include the following.

- Material whose disclosure would be '[likely to prejudice] the prevention or detection of crime, the apprehension or prosecution of offenders, or the assessment or collection of any tax or duty or of any imposition of a similar nature'.
- Data being used for management forecasting or planning, where it would harm that activity if the data were provided.
- The intentions of the data controller in regard to any negotiations with the data subject (so that you don't have to give away your negotiating position).
- Information that is subject to legal professional privilege (or the equivalent in Scotland) – for example advice you have received from your lawyer over a potential dismissal.
- Confidential references given *by* the data controller (see Chapter 13).

Note that there is *no* exemption for your organisation's opinions about the data subject. Where an opinion has been expressed by a third party there may be grounds for withholding it, under the third party provisions, but where it originates within your own organisation – for example a manager making comments on the performance of a member of their team – it must be shown.

As long as you are not infringing third party rights, you must also provide any information you have about the source of material in your records. For example, if you have received information from another organisation you may have to identify the organisation even if you do not identify the specific individual who provided it.

The subject access procedure

A subject access request must be made in writing. Although you cannot insist on the data subject using a specific form, you may find it worth preparing something like the example in Appendix C, to make the process easier both for you and for the data subject. A form can help to ensure that they provide you with all the information you need in order to comply promptly with the request. The process is shown schematically in Chart B.

You must also decide in advance whether you intend to charge for subject access or not. You are permitted to charge up to £10, regardless of how much material you hold. The policy in many organisations is not to charge for access by current or recent staff or volunteers. Others, for example, make a charge where a copy of the data is being provided, but not where it is merely being viewed (see below). You may want to charge for access by long-departed staff, just to reflect the additional work involved in retrieving their records.

You are allowed to refuse repeat applications that are unreasonably close together – for example if you know that the information is not likely to have changed in any significant way. With personnel records a reasonable interval could perhaps be as much as a year. It would be wise to use this provision sparingly, however, to avoid antagonising people unnecessarily.

You must be sure only to allow access by the right person: the data subject themselves or someone legitimately acting on their behalf. In the case of employees or volunteers who are familiar to your organisation, you may not need to insist on any identification documents at all. Where the access is from a past employee, or someone unfamiliar to the person who has responsibility for arranging the access, you would be wise to insist on a reasonable means of identification. You have to be satisfied that you are not contributing to a breach of security or confidentiality by providing access to the wrong person.

It is permissible for someone to act on behalf of the data subject – a solicitor or union official, for example – provided that (a) they have been properly authorised, and (b) they are acting in the data subject's interests. In the case of staff or volunteers it would normally be reasonable to insist on seeing a signed authorisation or other documentary evidence. No one has an automatic right to see another person's file – not even a parent on behalf of a child, for example. If the child is old enough to be working for you, whether paid or as a volunteer, they are likely to be old enough to exercise their own Data Protection rights. In Scotland, children are deemed capable of exercising their own Data Protection rights from the age of 12 in most cases. For England and Wales it depends, technically, on the individual child's understanding, but you can assume 12 to be about the age.

You are allowed to ask any reasonable questions that will help you locate the data. In the case of current staff or volunteers it is hard to see many cases when you would need this, but for past employees you may need to ask for a small amount of help, such as when they left the organisation. The questions must be ones that the data subject could be expected to answer ('What was your internal payroll number?' may be unreasonable), and even if they cannot answer the question, you must still try to find the data. You cannot refuse an access request just because an ex-volunteer can no longer remember whether it was May or June five years ago that they left. If the data subject cannot give you reasonable help, however, you are less likely to be penalised for failing to find their records.

Before responding to a subject access request, you may want to ask the data subject if there is anything particular they are hoping to see. Many Data Protection officers find that by negotiating over the scope of the access requested they can avoid spending time providing a lot of information that the data subject is not interested in, and can go straight to the document or part of the records that the request has been designed to elicit. If the data subject is satisfied with this partial access, you do not have to provide anything else, but of course they do have the right of access to the full record if they wish.

Having established what information the data subject wants to see, you should locate all the potentially relevant information and decide which of it is personal data. You should seek consent where you feel it is required from any third party and then exclude any data that you do not have to show because of one of the

Chart B: Subject access procedures

Note: If at any point you get stuck in a loop, you are not required to proceed any further.

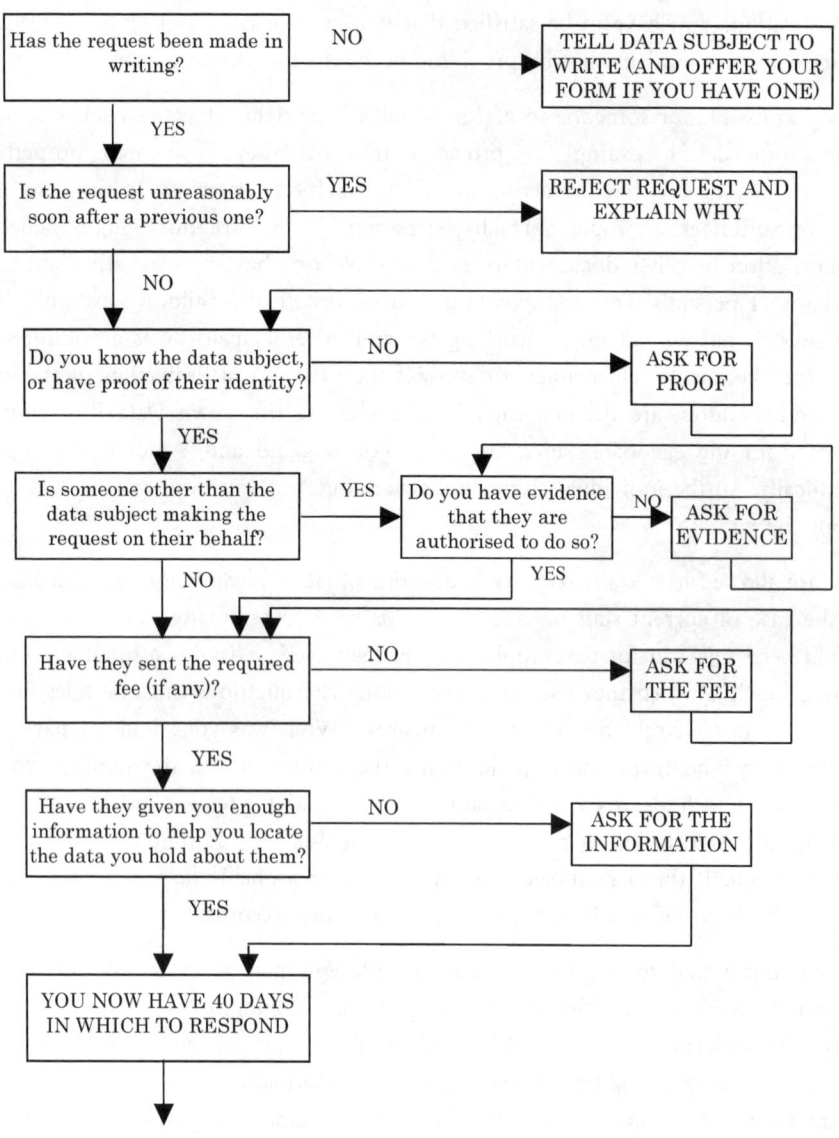

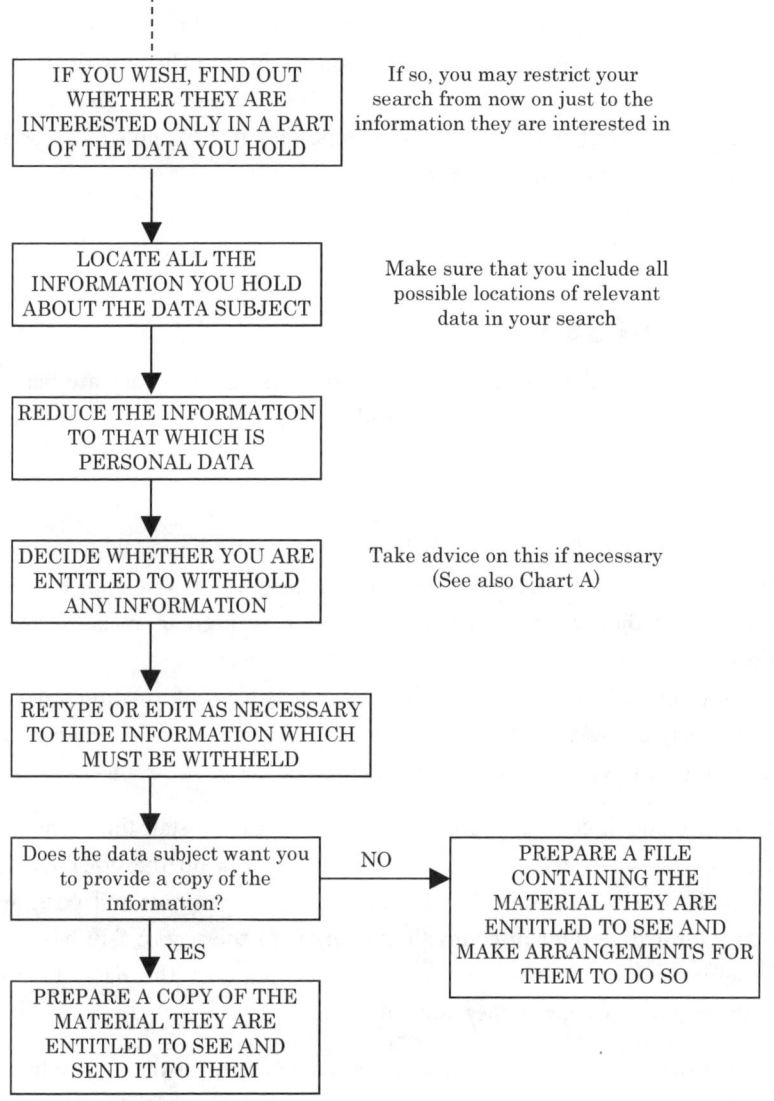

exemptions. This may involve editing or retyping a document so that you can show the relevant parts of it without infringing third party or other rights.

It cannot be over-emphasised that if you are in any doubt at all about what to show and what to withhold, or if it becomes obvious that the consequences of granting access to the data subject will be negative for the organisation (perhaps because a serious error will be brought to light) you should take legal advice in advance. You need to do this without delay, in order not to breach the 40-day time limit.

If you are being delayed by problems in making contact with third parties and are in danger of missing the 40-day deadline, you should provide access to as much of the data as you can in the meantime and explain the situation to the data subject.

If the data subject is not satisfied that you have granted them the full access they are entitled to, they can ask the Court to order you to do so. (This was the basis of the 'Durant' case: see Glossary and page 15.) Data subjects are unlikely to accept being fobbed off with a sketchy response, especially if they know or suspect that a particular document is in your records.

Providing access

The data subject is entitled to receive a copy of the personal data they are being given access to. You are not obliged to provide a copy of the data if the data subject doesn't want one, and some data controllers encourage the data subject just to view the data instead.

You should consider carefully where the balance of advantage lies. Making a copy will inevitably incur a cost, in time and materials. However, if it is difficult for the data subject to visit the personnel department you may need to make a copy anyway in order to provide access at a more convenient location, so you might as well just provide the copy straight to the data subject. Where information is held on computer it may be awkward to allow one data subject to view their own data without disclosing others', whereas a print-out may be easier to arrange.

Equally, if you provide direct access this will also incur costs in staff time, since it is unwise to provide unsupervised access. Supervised access, on the other hand, does give you the opportunity to explain things, answer questions, and possibly even provide a limited amount of counselling along with the access. You have to choose the approach that is best for you, remembering that the data subject always has the right to a copy if they want it.

The only exceptions to providing a 'copy in permanent form' if the data subject wants one are where this is either not possible, or would require 'disproportionate effort' on the part of the data controller. In either case, however, the data subject still has a right of access – in other words they must be able to inspect the data.

It is important to note that the data subject is entitled to a copy of the *information*, not necessarily of the actual *documents* in which the information is held. There may be cases where it is more sensible to retype the relevant parts of a document, rather than photocopying it. Where hand-written notes have been made, for example, or where there are significant parts of the information that may legitimately be withheld, this may be the best option.

The data must be communicated 'in an intelligible form'. This means, for example, that any codes that may appear in a print-out from the computer system must be explained. It may be worth preparing a standard glossary for all codes used in the system, and possibly for esoteric technical terms as well, rather than providing specific explanations each time there is an access request.

The intelligibility requirement, reinforced by the Disability Discrimination Act 1995, suggests that an employer may have to consider 'reasonable adjustments' when providing access to the data for an employee. This could mean providing key documents in a format that is appropriate to the data subject – in large print, for example.

Having made a copy you must then ensure that it ends up in the right hands. Where the data subject is easily available, it is usually best to hand it directly to them. Where this is not practicable, and you need to post it, you should:

■ check that you have the right address;
■ confirm with the data subject that they are happy for you to post it – if they live in a building with shared postal arrangements they might not regard the post as secure enough, or you might decide to use a signed-for service;
■ mark the envelope 'Private and confidential'.

If you have withheld material you do not have to tell the data subject so, although you may if you wish and if you don't feel that it will only encourage them to come back and ask for the missing material – or it may be obvious if you have blanked out third party identifying details. Your covering letter might say something like, 'Here is all the material which we are required to provide you with in response to your subject access request.' You should provide them with details of a contact person in case they have any questions or comments on the material.

Where you are providing direct access rather than providing a copy, you must supervise the data subject throughout. While most data subjects are likely to be trustworthy, it is far more equitable to supervise everyone rather than to try to make a judgement about who might tamper with the information or try to remove documents. (It has happened.) For this, you obviously need to arrange a private room or area where the data subject and the person supervising will be reasonably comfortable and undisturbed. You may also want to ensure that facilities are available so that a copy can be made there and then of anything the data subject wants copied.

Recording subject access

Whenever anyone makes a subject access request it is important to keep a record of how you have responded. This should contain the following.

- The original written application, along with evidence of the data subject's identity and/or authorisation for someone to act on their behalf.
- Details of which record systems you have examined for data relating to that person, in order to show that you have looked properly.
- A list of what you sent or showed the person (with enough information to identify documents unambiguously), together with evidence of the date you sent it, or the date they viewed the records. (If the amount of information provided is small, or if it consists mainly of printouts from electronic systems, it may be easier to keep a copy of what was sent, rather than a list.)
- A copy of both the edited and unedited versions of any material that was provided in redacted form.
- A list of any information that was withheld.
- A record of any consent from third parties, sought, given or refused.
- A record of any advice you have taken on what to show or withhold.
- A record of the reasons why you have withheld material, or provided third party material without consent, and a record of who in your organisation authorised this action.

If the data subject believes that you have not complied with their subject access request properly they may complain to you, and you may want to review your actions. They may also complain to the Information Commissioner, and you would then need to be able to show exactly what you had done and why.

You should keep your file relating to the subject access request until there is no likelihood of the data subject complaining. A reasonable length of time would probably be six months to a year. This length of retention would also help you decide whether you have grounds for refusing a subsequent request on the grounds that it is unreasonably soon.

Publicising the right of access

Rights will only be used if people know about them. While you may not want to encourage speculative or frivolous subject access requests, it is good practice to make sure that your staff are made reasonably well aware of their subject access rights.

You may want to do this:

- at the time of application or appointment, where you are collecting significant amounts of information;
- during induction;
- in the staff handbook, or on the organisation's intranet;

- whenever you ask people to check that you have the right information about them;
- when people leave – at which point you may also want to tell them what sort of information you will be retaining about them, and for how long you will keep it.

For those who are interested in pursuing their right of subject access you should have a clear statement of the procedure which is easily accessible (along with a form, if you have one), mentioning any charge you make for some or all data subjects. If you also have an open files policy you should explain the difference between that type of access to the files and a formal subject access request.

Chapter summary

Subject access under the Data Protection Act is compatible with an open files policy, but the two must be kept distinct.

Anyone on whom a record is kept may apply for access, and is entitled – subject to certain exceptions – to be given a copy of all the personal data that was held about them at they time they made the application. The main exceptions are for matters which are in train, such as negotiations, and 'third party' material (where someone else is the source or the subject of the information).

Subject access compliance can be complicated, and the outcome for the organisation can be serious, either if it fails to comply fully, or if the information that must be disclosed reflects badly on the organisation. In all but straightforward cases, it is wise to consider taking legal advice, before any irrevocable steps are taken.

Document	Main requirements	Retention period	File location
Record of subject access request	Demonstrate how request was answered	One year	Data Protection officer

chapter 8

RECRUITMENT AND SELECTION

The recruitment and selection process is about defining clearly what job you want done, then finding the best possible person to fill it. Your record-keeping must be related to carrying out these tasks, and to proving that you have done them properly.

You need to demonstrate that you have given all candidates a fair chance to demonstrate their suitability for the post, and that you have treated them all fairly at each stage of the process. You must also be able to show that you have complied with all the legal requirements not to discriminate (see Appendix A) – particularly in your job descriptions, person specifications, arrangements for interviewing, shortlisting, the interview itself, making the decision, and the appointment process.

In relation to applicants with disabilities you must make 'reasonable adjustments' to enable people to apply, to attend interviews and to carry out the job if appointed. The requirement not to discriminate on grounds of disability now applies to all employers whatever their staff size.

You should not use the recruitment process to collect information that will only be applicable to the employment relationship between you and the successful candidate. That can wait.

The documents we are concerned with here are:

- the job description;
- the person specification;
- the job advertisement;
- the information sent out to enquirers;
- the application form;
- monitoring and vetting forms;
- records of the short-listing process;
- records of interviews and any other selection procedures;
- the letters sent to unsuccessful candidates;
- the letter sent to the successful candidate;
- references;
- results of CRB or other checks.

You should consider offering this information in alternative formats – for example in large print, in Braille, on disc or on tape – without waiting for a prospective applicant to ask. These provisions are often likely to be taken as a 'reasonable adjustment' to the needs of someone with a disability, particularly if your information systems, and the time available before the new employee is needed, mean it can easily be done. There is no requirement to make 'reasonable adjustments' for volunteer posts, but it is obviously good practice.

Information about the job

Any job description must spell out clearly what the job entails, so that potential applicants can see clearly whether it is appropriate for them or not. Writing good job descriptions is not easy, but should not be skimped (see below). Changing a job description after the event, or asking someone to carry out duties that differ significantly from their job description can give rise to considerable managerial and legal difficulties.

The main purpose of a person specification is to give those responsible for selection a set of objective criteria on which to judge applications and to give those applying for posts the opportunity to see how well they meet the criteria. The best person specifications have criteria that are clearly related to the demands of the job, are measurable or testable, and do not introduce unjustifiable criteria.

You must keep copies of all the information that candidates see before applying for the job, until the post has been filled. The job description and person specification should be dated and added to the post-holder's file. It is usually also necessary to have a central file of all current job information. This should, of course, be updated whenever a job description or person specification is changed (See Chapter 9 for more on the possible contractual implications of changing someone's job description.)

There is no reason why job information should be confidential, as a job description and person specification relate to the *post*, not the *person*. Other staff may well need to look up their colleagues' areas of responsibility, while line managers will need to refer to them in the context of supervision and appraisal. Job information may have to be attached to funding applications for specific posts, and will also be required if you ever carry out a job evaluation exercise.

Job advertisements, equally, are not confidential, but there is generally no requirement to keep them available after a post has been filled. If they are retained for future reference, in case the post becomes vacant again, they should be held by the personnel department.

The advertisement

The job advertisement (or different versions in different publications) must be an accurate summary of the most significant parts of both the job description and person specification. If you eventually offer someone a job that differs significantly from the information you sent out, you will at best risk them turning the job down, and wasting your recruitment effort. At worst you might find yourself contractually committed to something you did not intend.

You may find the following checklist for an advertisement helpful:

- your organisation's name and logo;
- the job title;
- where the job is based;
- a general idea of the duties involved and any qualifications required;
- the salary;
- a brief equal opportunities statement (such as 'Our organisation works within Equal Opportunities Principles');
- whether the job is open to job sharing;
- the closing date and date of interview;
- how to get further details – e-mail, phone, address, web site;
- registered charity number and company number.

Include the following if they apply:

- the duration of post if it is for a fixed term;
- the hours if it is not full-time;
- a statement of any positive action being taken;
- a reference to any Genuine Occupational Requirements that apply;
- the 'double-tick' disability symbol (see Glossary) if you are signed up for it;
- any level of CRB disclosure required.

If you recruit through an agency, in particular, bear in mind the Data Protection requirement to inform potential applicants about who they are providing their information to (see box below).

Information Commissioner's benchmarks on advertisements

1   Inform individuals responding to job advertisements of the name of the organisation to which they will be providing their information and how it will be used unless this is self-evident

2   Recruitment agencies, used on behalf of an employer, must identify themselves and explain how personal data they receive will be used and disclosed unless this is self-evident.

> 3 On receiving identifiable particulars of applicants from an agency ensure, as soon as you can, that the applicants are aware of the name of the organisation now holding their information.

Job descriptions

The job description should be reviewed each time you recruit for the post. Job descriptions will be specific to each organisation, but the typical format is that:

- they should state clearly and simply the duties, tasks, responsibilities and lines of accountability of the post-holder;
- they should begin with the job title, who the post is responsible to and who the post is responsible for, then the main purpose of the job in one or two short paragraphs;
- the next section(s) cover the tasks in the job bunched under main headings, with a final section to cover general duties;
- no job description should be more than three sides of A4;
- wording should be precise, when it matters – for example, 'ensure' means that the post-holder does not normally do the task themselves; they supervise the person who does it, and take over in an emergency; 'control' means that they set up a system and issue instructions to colleagues.

Person specifications

It is good practice to derive a person specification for all posts.

The person specification should list the characteristics a person needs to carry out the job. These are typically listed under six main headings.

- Experience
- Knowledge
- Skills
- Abilities
- Education/Training and Qualifications
- Special Requirements

The person specification should derive from the job description. Each requirement must be justifiable in relation to one or more tasks from the job description, and must not be discriminatory or excessive. Each requirement must also be measurable or testable in some way, whether on the application form, during the interview or through a particular test such as a typing test. You should generally end up with between ten and fifteen criteria, or fewer for less demanding posts. See the Resources section (page 190) for where to find guidance on drawing up person specifications.

Before moving on to draw up your application form you must decide how you are going to assess each requirement in the person specification. Some will be best covered at interview, others by direct testing (such as word-processing ability, for example), or by a combination. For those being tested on the application form, you will need to devise questions to identify as clearly as possible whether the applicant meets the requirement or not.

Other information sent out to enquirers

It is good practice for the covering letter to enquirers to:

■ be personalised;
■ remind applicants of the closing date;
■ state the interview dates if known;
■ tell applicants whether you will acknowledge the receipt of their form or not;
■ point out the equal opportunities monitoring form and give full reasons for why it is included;
■ say when they can expect to hear if they are shortlisted, and whether they will hear from you at all if they are not shortlisted;
■ say whether there will be an opportunity to visit your office before the interview if they are shortlisted;
■ be clear about how to fill in the application form;
■ point out any disclosures the applicant is required to make, and any vetting checks that you will carry out (such as with the CRB).

You should also send some (but not too much) general information about your organisation and the specific project, where relevant. It needs to cover:

■ the mission statement and structure of the organisation;
■ any relevant information about the team or project the person would be working for, including hard information such as statistics and details of clients or users as appropriate;
■ a description of any access restrictions for any buildings the person would be using;
■ your equal opportunities statement.

More information, such as the most recent annual report, can be sent to shortlisted candidates.

Don't forget to make all your materials available in alternative formats unless there is a very good reason not to.

The application form

The only real purpose of the application form is to enable you to assess whether applicants appear to meet the criteria on the person specification. Although you will undoubtedly have to use the application form to collect other information to assist you with the recruitment process – for example the applicant's contact details – do not use it for collecting any information that is not relevant at this stage of the process. For example, you should not normally ask about the applicant's family, National Insurance details or trade union membership.

In particular, do not ask for any information about health or disabilities, unless it is directly relevant to the person specification. Because this information is 'sensitive' under the Data Protection Act 1998, if you do need to ask for it you must explain fully how you will use the information, and why it is relevant.

Questions about criminal convictions should not be asked as a matter of course, but included only when necessary, following the exemptions in the Rehabilitation of Offenders Act 1974. These include most health professions, work in education, social work or child protection, and accountancy posts (see Appendix A).

For certain jobs you are required to carry out CRB checks on previous criminal convictions, as well as obtaining proof of identity and evidence of the applicant's employment history and qualifications. This applies to all posts (paid and unpaid) in places that are:

- required to register under the Registered Homes Act 1984 (as amended);
- required to register under the Care Standards Act 2000;
- providing young people under 18 with accommodation, care or social services;
- working with vulnerable adults.

Even where you are not required to verify the information provided you will nearly always want to do so. Your form should explain how you will do this, and whether you intend to contact anyone at this stage. If so, you should get the applicant's consent in the case of their current employer. See also the Information Commissioner's benchmarks, below.

Your checklist for an application form should:

- identify your organisation and the post being applied for;

- ask for details of how you can contact the applicant, by post, phone and, if you wish, fax or e-mail – if time is limited, specify the dates at which you might need to contact them and give them the option of supplying alternatives;
- give the applicant an opportunity to provide full information which demonstrates how they meet all your requirements;
- be careful only to ask for information which is relevant to the short-listing stage of the application;
- not ask for health, disability or criminal conviction information unless it is necessary to the post, and if you do ask for it, explain clearly why;
- explain any checks you will carry out on the information;
- get consent for any verification that will involve you asking other parties for documents relating to the applicant, or for contacting their current employer;
- impress on the applicant that they must provide truthful information, and ask them to sign that they have done so;
- provide a distinctively marked envelope for the return of applications, so that you can handle them confidentially when they arrive, or a specific e-mail address to ensure that applications go directly to an appropriate person who will handle them confidentially.

Normal good practice is to design an application form that is specific to each job. This has the advantage that you can ask very direct questions relating to each requirement in the person specification. This makes the applicant's task easier, and they will be less likely to overlook crucial information that might affect your decision. A sample form that follows this approach is given in Appendix D.

The alternative is to design a standard form just with main headings that match the headings in your person specification format, and ask applicants to demonstrate in each section how they meet the requirements. Your form could say something like: 'Please read the person specification for this job carefully, then explain under each heading how you meet all the requirements'.

If your personnel department is over-stretched, you might have to take the generic option. In most cases, however, you will get a better quality of response by designing a new application form (based on many common elements, of course) for each job.

See also the discussion towards the end of this chapter on how to avoid transferring excessive information to the successful applicant's eventual personnel file.

Information Commissioner's benchmarks on application forms

1 State, on any application form, to whom the information is being provided and how it will be used if this is not self-evident.

2 Only seek personal data that are relevant to the recruitment decision to be made.

3 Only request information about an applicant's criminal convictions if that information can be justified in terms of the role offered. If this information is justified, make it clear that spent convictions do not have to be declared, unless the job being filled is covered by the Exceptions Order to the Rehabilitation of Offenders Act 1974.

4 Explain any checks that might be undertaken to verify the information provided in the application form including the nature of additional sources from which information may be gathered. (The verification checks should meet the benchmarks set out in the next section.)

5 If sensitive data are collected ensure a sensitive data condition is satisfied.

6 Provide a secure method for sending applications.

Equal opportunities monitoring form

A monitoring form is normally part of the application pack and is sent to all candidates. Several of the common monitoring categories are 'sensitive data', in terms of the Data Protection Act, so you need to be particularly careful in how you approach this. Normally, the use of sensitive data requires 'explicit' consent but there are exemptions for some monitoring categories. There are roughly three possibilities.

■ The category is not sensitive, so you do not need consent. These include age and gender.

■ The category is sensitive, but there is special provision so that you do not need consent. These are racial or ethnic origin, religion and disability.

■ The category is sensitive and there is no special provision, so that you cannot collect or use the information without consent. These include sexuality and criminal record.

Provision for use of data on racial or ethnic origin for monitoring is made in Schedule 3 of the Data Protection Act. Provision for use of data on disability or religion is made in the Data Protection (Processing of Sensitive Personal Data) Order 2000 (SI 2000 No. 417). The precise conditions vary slightly between the two pieces of legislation but it is more convenient to follow the good practice recommendations in the text above, which make no distinction.

You cannot force someone to complete a monitoring form by making it a condition of considering their application. It is unlikely that you could show this to be compliant with the first Data Protection Principle (see Chapter 3). However, there are many reasons why you might want to encourage people to respond, both for your own internal processes and possibly for external funders.

Although there are some cases where anonymous monitoring is sufficient and more likely to encourage a response, in the case of job applications you normally want to track people through the process. A discrepancy between the proportions of male applicants and male interviewees, for example, might indicate bias in your process.

The difficulty is how to identify people while maintaining confidentiality. A common approach is to have the monitoring form as a separate sheet, but with either the applicant's name or a reference number to link it back to the main application. This sheet could be submitted completely separately, perhaps in a sealed envelope accompanying the application, or it can be separated out immediately the application is received. Analysis of the monitoring forms should be carried out as a distinct activity, ideally by someone not involved in the selection process, and the results should only be released, even internally, as figures which do not allow individuals to be identified.

In order to encourage the maximum response, your monitoring form should give a full explanation of why you are carrying out monitoring and why it is not being done anonymously, and it should describe the process by which you will maintain confidentiality. (See the sample monitoring form in Appendix D.) At the same time, you must make it clear that a response is not mandatory. You should either say that people may choose to ignore one or more questions, or you should have a 'Prefer not to say' option for each question.

While you are free to choose your own descriptions, you may find it easier to use standard categories. The Commission for Racial Equality (CRE) recommends using the categories of the 2001 census or an expanded set that can be mapped to the same main categories. You can refine the categories to reflect local circumstances, either by adding groups, or collapsing groups to three or four main categories. For more detailed advice see the CRE web site (see the Resources section on page 186).

Information Commissioner's benchmarks on equal opportunities monitoring

1 Information about a worker's ethnic origin, disability or religion is sensitive personal data. Ensure that equal opportunities monitoring of these characteristics satisfies a sensitive data condition.

2 Only use information that identifies individual workers where this is necessary to carry out meaningful equal opportunities monitoring. Where practicable, keep the information collected in an anonymised form.

3 Ensure questions are designed so that so that the personal information collected through them is accurate and not excessive.

The application process up to shortlisting

Before starting out on a recruitment process, you should be clear about how you are going to handle the records it generates. Any information about individuals should be treated as confidential. (Even casual enquirers about the post may not want anyone to know they are looking around.) This means that all stages of the process should be carried out by specified people only, who have been made aware of the need for confidentiality.

There is usually no need to keep a record of who has enquired. In fact it is often easiest to have a set of envelopes ready to send out, and to transfer the name and address directly to the envelope when someone phones up, e-mails or writes in. The e-mail can then be deleted, or the letter destroyed. If a list is made, perhaps so that information packs can be sent out in a batch, this should be subsequently destroyed.

It is best for information packs to include an envelope for those who want to apply on paper. These should be distinctively marked, so that they can be handled confidentially when they arrive.

For applications by e-mail it is essential that they should be received only by the person handling the recruitment process. Depending on your set-up it may be relatively easy to create a separate e-mail address to which applications are to be sent, with restricted access, or you may wish to specify a particular person to receive them. If applications have to go to a general address which other people also use, it may be necessary to restrict access to this, so that the responsible person is always the one to initiate the 'send and receive' process, and can remove applications before allowing others to access the e-mail system.

Once applications are received, the monitoring forms should be detached and kept securely, while the application forms themselves must, obviously, also be kept securely. Many organisations nowadays keep all personal information on the front page of an application form that can be numbered and detached from the body of the form, but referenced back to it if the applicant is shortlisted. The main body of the form only is then provided to those doing the shortlisting. This is to try to prevent any unfair discrimination resulting from shortlisters making assumptions about a person's suitability on the basis of their age, race, gender or other personal criteria.

If you need to send copies of application forms out to the shortlisting panel, they should be instructed on how to treat these confidentially. For example, you may assume that people would know not to read application forms on the train where other people can overlook them, but this does happen. The panel should also be told to return their copies of the applications afterwards for you to destroy, so that you know this has been done, and this should be followed up if necessary.

Shortlisting

Shortlisting should use a standard form where each member of the panel first makes their own separate assessment of how closely each applicant matches the criteria in the person specification. (See example in Appendix F.) The assessments should then be compared to produce an agreed outcome from the panel. The assessment forms should be returned and kept with the application forms so that you can demonstrate consistency of treatment (while allowing for individual differences of judgement between panel members, of course).

After you have shortlisted, you will need to write, inviting candidates to interview. At this point you must be sure to ask if there are any special provisions you need to make to enable them to attend. This could be anything such as a reserved parking space with easy access to your building, an induction loop in the room being used for the interview, or particularly detailed travel directions, for example.

In most voluntary organisations there will be no need to make use of automatic systems for sifting applications or of psychometric or other tests. If for any reason you do want to use these, you must ensure that you tell applicants about them, and that you use them appropriately and in a way that is not discriminatory.

Information Commissioner's benchmarks on shortlisting

1   Be consistent in the way personal data are used in the process of short-listing candidates for a particular position.

2   Inform applicants if an automated short-listing system will be used as the sole basis for making a decision. Make provisions to consider representations from applicants about this and to take these into account before making the final decision.

3   Ensure that tests based on the interpretation of scientific evidence, such as psychological tests and handwriting analysis, are only used and interpreted by those who have received appropriate training.

Interviews

This is clearly not the place to go into detail on how to conduct interviews. The essential points in the context of this book are to:

- ask only for information that is relevant to the post;
- treat all candidates consistently;
- give candidates an opportunity to comment on any other information you have obtained as part of the process (for example if you cannot verify some of the information given on their application form);
- keep records of any information given that will be used in reaching the interview panel's decision.
- keep records of the decision-making process, to show that it is fair.

At some interviews, candidates may have to be asked to disclose or discuss information about their criminal record or other 'sensitive' data. The chair of the panel should ensure that these questions, in particular, can be fully justified and that the answers are accurately recorded.

You must be able to show that the panel treated everyone fairly by obtaining and recording all the information they could that was relevant to their decision, and then making a fair choice on the basis of the information. If they cannot justify the decision objectively, you may be open to a challenge on the basis of discrimination.

For this reason all the notes taken by every member of the interview panel must be collected in afterwards and stored securely, along with any summary sheets prepared during the panel's deliberations. Panel members should be told at the outset that this will happen, and must be told (or ideally trained) to take objective and fair notes in a way that is consistent for all candidates.

Information Commissioner's benchmarks on interviewing

1 Ensure that personal data that are recorded and retained following interview can be justified as relevant to, and necessary for, the recruitment process itself, or for defending the process against challenge

Pre-employment checks: general considerations

In general you should only obtain information about a candidate with their knowledge and at the most appropriate stage of the recruitment process. In most voluntary organisations it will normally make sense to leave any checking until after the interviews, and then only to carry out checks on the person you intend to appoint (remembering, of course, to make the job offer subject to satisfactory references and other checks). This is cheaper and less effort for you, as well as less intrusive for the unsuccessful candidates. Among the checks you are most likely to carry out are:

- references from previous employers or others who know the candidate, to confirm the information they have provided you with and to give you information about them which is not obtainable in any other way;
- confirmation of claimed qualifications and professional status, from educational institutions or professional bodies;
- checks on eligibility to work in the UK;
- CRB checks.

You should not be afraid of making these checks if they are necessary. While it is comforting to believe that most people are honest, the voluntary sector is by no means immune from people who misrepresent themselves or lie outright in order to obtain jobs they are unsuited for. It is far better to weed these people out during the recruitment process, than to appoint the wrong person and then have to deal with a dismissal.

So there is often a good reason – even a requirement – to make these checks, but they must be proportionate. There may be no need, for example, to check the professional qualifications of someone who is going to be working for you in a capacity that is not related to their profession.

Generally these checks involve you in obtaining information from other sources, in order to confirm what the candidate has told you. Unless the source is publicly available (such as a list of people registered to practise a particular profession), you should normally get the individual's consent for you to approach the source and for the source to disclose the information. This should normally be in writing, so that you have evidence if required.

The easiest way to get consent is on your application form, where you should explain what checks you will carry out, and ask for the applicant's signed consent for you to do so at the appropriate time. (See the sample form in Appendix D.) In other cases there may be a prescribed way of demonstrating consent (such as on the CRB form).

When approaching any source for information you should spell out exactly what information you are seeking, and you should be careful only to ask for information which is clearly relevant to your requirements. As far as possible you should ask for factual information, or opinions that can be backed up by factual information. General assertions of someone's suitability for a post, for example, which are hard to substantiate, are likely to be far less useful to you and more likely to be unfair to the individual.

References and CRB disclosures must be treated as highly confidential (even if the candidate will get the chance to see the contents). You should ask for references to be sent to a named individual in an envelope marked 'Confidential', or provide a reply envelope that is distinctively marked to that it will not be opened inadvertently. Those handling the post should be given clear instructions to deliver the items to the responsible person unopened. Similarly, do not ask for a reference by e-mail unless you are sure it can be handled confidentially, and avoid asking for a faxed reference unless the need is genuinely urgent and you can arrange for the responsible person to be standing by the machine as the fax comes through.

No one, other than possibly the candidate, should be allowed to see a reference or CRB disclosure unless they have a genuine need in connection with the recruitment process. An enhanced CRB check may contain a special category of information that is released by the police only to the authorised counter-signatory. Such information is highly restricted, and even its existence must not be revealed without written permission from the police. See the Resources section (page 184) for the disclosure web site, which offers more on this subject.

It is very unlikely that you will need to carry out vetting for a voluntary organisation post. 'Vetting' is where you collect additional information from a variety of people about the character and background of a candidate to reassure yourself that they are trustworthy and suitable for particular responsibilities. Should you find it necessary, the Information Commissioner's benchmarks are given here.

Information Commissioner's benchmarks on verification

1 Explain to applicants as early as is reasonably practicable in the recruitment process the nature of the verification process and the methods used to carry it out.

2 If it is necessary to secure the release of documents or information from a third party, obtain a signed consent form from the applicant unless consent to their release has been indicated in some other way.

3 Give the applicant an opportunity to make representations should any of the checks produce discrepancies.

Information Commissioner's benchmarks on pre-employment vetting

1 Only use vetting where there are particular and significant risks to the employer, clients, customers or others, and where there is no less intrusive and reasonably practicable alternative.

2 Only carry out pre-employment vetting on an applicant at an appropriate point in the recruitment process. Comprehensive vetting should only be conducted on a successful applicant.

3 Make it clear early in the recruitment process that vetting will take place and how it will be conducted.

4 Only use vetting as a means of obtaining specific information, not as a means of general intelligence gathering. Ensure that the extent and nature of information sought is justified

5 Only seek information from sources where it is likely that relevant information will be revealed. Only approach the applicant's family or close associates in exceptional cases.

6 Do not place reliance on information collected from possibly unreliable sources. Allow the applicant to make representations regarding information that will affect the decision to finally appoint.

7 Where information is collected about a third party, e.g. the applicant's partner, ensure so far as practicable that the third party is made aware of this.

8 If it is necessary to secure the release of documents or information from a third party, obtain a signed consent form from the applicant.

Proof of entitlement to work

The Asylum and Immigration Act 1996 as amended in 2004 requires all employers in the UK to make basic document checks on every person they intend to employ. The Home Office web site publishes comprehensive guidance for UK employers on preventing illegal working; there is also a helpline (see the Resources section on page 185). If you employ someone who is not entitled to work in the UK, having failed to make the checks (or in the knowledge that they are not entitled to work in the UK), you can be fined up to £5,000. The checks provide a 'statutory defence' against breaking the law, and should be made before a person starts working for you. The current position applies for all employees taken on after 30 April 2004. You do not need to apply these document checks to employees taken on before that date; in most cases you should have already made checks under the previous system.

For every new employee you must (a) see, (b) check and (c) copy either one or two documents to prove their entitlement to work in the UK (see Appendix A for lists of the relevant documents). The documents must be originals, not copies.

You must take 'reasonable steps' to check that the documents appear genuine. The Home Office guidance is that you must, in particular:

- check that photographs appear to be of the prospective employee;
- check that dates of birth are consistent with the apparent age of the person;
- check that expiry dates have not been passed;
- check that UK government stamps or endorsements do allow the type of work you are offering;
- get a third document (such as a marriage certificate) to explain the reason if the two documents produced are in different names.

You must make a copy of the relevant parts of the documents. These are: the front cover and all the pages which give your prospective employee's personal details, especially the photograph and signature; and any page containing a UK government stamp or endorsement which allows the person to do the work you are offering.

The copy can be either a photocopy or an electronic copy. If you want to scan the documents and keep them electronically you must record them in a form which cannot subsequently be tampered with (for example on a read-only CD). You should not hold on to a person's documents for longer than it takes to copy them, and certainly no more than a day.

You must keep the copies of the documents for as long as you are employing a person and for at least three years after they have left. The information in the documents that you copy is, of course, highly personal and should be kept very confidential. You should not use the information you collect in this way for any purpose other than to demonstrate that you have carried out the necessary checks, in the event that the question arises. It may well, therefore, be appropriate to store it away from the personnel files, in a separate location with additional security.

When you make these checks it is very important that you do not introduce an element of discrimination. You should treat all the documents that fall into the same category as of equal value, and you should treat all applicants alike. Do not assume, for example, that a white person who has been educated in this country and sounds 'English' (or Welsh, Scottish or Irish) is automatically entitled to work here; you must see, check and copy their documentary proof of this just as you would for anyone else.

The need to check a document may introduce some delay into the recruitment process. It could constitute unlawful racial discrimination if you were to reject a candidate because the document they produced was more difficult to read or understand, or would take longer to check.

You should make it clear from the outset that you will require approved documents, but you should not ask for these until you really need them. This will normally be on appointment, and not before. If you ask for proof at any earlier stage, you will be collecting unnecessarily intrusive information about those applicants who are eventually unsuccessful, and there could always be the suspicion that their status might have affected your decision.

People from eight of the countries which joined the European Union on 1 May 2004 are entitled to work freely in the UK, but must register with the Home Office. These countries are the Czech Republic, Estonia, Hungary, Latvia, Lithuania, Poland, Slovakia and Slovenia. You are responsible for ensuring that they register within one month of starting work, and you must keep the copy of the registration certificate which is issued to you by the Home Office. This should be kept with the other proof of entitlement to work.

Criminal Records checks

You will – or certainly should – already know whether any posts in your organisation require CRB checks, and the level of disclosure that applies. The CRB has a Code of Practice, more detailed than the Information Commissioner's benchmarks, on how to handle, process and store information obtained under CRB checks. This can be found on the CRB web site (see the Resources section on page 184).

The Code of Practice applies to 'registered persons'. This includes organisations that receive disclosure information (either on their own behalf or via an umbrella body) and individuals who countersign disclosure applications or who see the information as part of the recruitment process. It is worth noting that the legislation and the Code of Practice refer to 'registered persons' while the CRB web site and the disclosure web site talk about 'registered bodies'; it is never made clear that these are, in fact, the same thing.

Under the Code, your organisation must have *written* policies covering:

- fair treatment in the employment of ex-offenders; and
- the correct handling and safe-keeping of disclosure information.

Most of the provisions in the Code are simply good practice, and are consistent with the principles which have been discussed elsewhere in this book.

People applying for jobs where a CRB check will be made must be told that this will happen, and must be given a copy of your policy on the fair treatment of ex-offenders, on request. They must also be reassured on the application form or supporting material that you will not discriminate against them unfairly: you have to say explicitly that a previous conviction will not necessarily be a bar to their employment. If you make a conditional offer of employment but then want to withdraw it as a result of a CRB check, you must discuss the matter with the individual first.

You must make guidance on the fair treatment of ex-offenders available to those involved in appointing staff, specifically with reference to the Rehabilitation of Offenders Act 1974. You must also:

- ensure that the information is not passed to anyone who is not authorised to receive it – unauthorised disclosure is an offence;
- ensure that disclosures, and the information they contain, are available only to those who need to have access in the course of their duties;
- securely store disclosures and the information that they contain.

The Code says that you should normally not keep any information about the content of a disclosure for longer than six months. It does, however, allow the period to be exceeded in 'very exceptional circumstances'. Organisations subject to Care Standards are obliged to keep the content of CRB disclosures until after the next inspection. While this approach may seem at odds with the CRB Code and with good Data Protection practice (because the information will no longer be up to date), non-compliance with Commission for Social Care Inspection (CSCI) expectations could have very serious consequences. You may want to regard this as 'very exceptional circumstances'.

If your organisation acts as an umbrella body you are responsible for ensuring that organisations which make CRB checks through you follow the Code of Practice.

> **Information Commissioner's benchmarks on handling of information obtained through CRB disclosure**
>
> 1 Consider carefully whether it is necessary for the protection or conduct of business to request a disclosure. The collection and holding of disclosure information that is excessive will breach the data protection principles.
> 2 Once disclosure information has been obtained and an employment decision made, do not retain the information unless there is an overriding reason for doing so. Usually it will be sufficient to record that the check has been carried out and its result. In any event, do not retain the information for more than 6 months.
> 3 Do not share with other employers the information obtained through a disclosure.
> 4 Do not attempt to obtain information about criminal convictions by enforced subject access or from sources other than the CRB or the applicant. The carrying out of media checks to look for spent convictions for a post that is not eligible for standard or enhanced disclosure is likely to breach the Act. Media checks involve obtaining information from old newspaper articles or similar sources about an individual.

Checks under the Care Standards Act 2000

Under the Care Standards Act 2000 there is an obligation to obtain certain information about all staff, paid and unpaid, in care homes, children's homes, health care organisations, residential family centres, domiciliary care agencies and nursing agencies. All staff must have a satisfactory either standard or enhanced CRB check (depending on their post).

For new staff you must also get:

- proof of identity, including a recent photograph;
- documentary evidence of any relevant qualifications;
- two references (for some posts one or both of these must be from the most recent employer(s), if any).

For some posts (but not all) you must obtain:

- birth certificate and current passport (if any);

- a full employment history, with satisfactory written explanations of any gaps;
- verification (so far as reasonably practicable) of why previous employment involving work with children or vulnerable adults ended.

For more details, the CSCI web site (see the Resources section on page 184) gives a list of the National Minimum Standards for different types of service provider, under 'Information for service providers'.

The National Minimum Standards that apply to your area of work may make specific requirements about personnel record-keeping. For example, those for children's homes say that you must have:

'... a written record of the recruitment process which is followed in respect of all staff (including ancillary staff and those on a contractual/sessional basis) and volunteers who work with children in the home, including evidence that all requirements of Schedule 2 of the SI 2001 No. 3967 have been met in every case.'

Where a person is employed by an agency or is a secondee you must be satisfied that the employing organisation has obtained all relevant information.

References

You should always make the request for a reference in writing, and ask for a written response. Your letter should make it clear that the candidate has consented to the disclosure of information about them to you. You should be prepared to provide the evidence of this if necessary, although your assertion that you have obtained consent will often be sufficient. Your letter should also specify whether you are asking for a confidential reference – which the individual will not be allowed to see later on, under a subject access request (see Chapter 5) – or an open reference which they *will* be allowed to see. It is often best to ask for an open reference but to give the referee the option, as a last resort, of providing it in confidence if that is what they feel they need to do. (See the sample reference request letter in Appendix E.)

You should never act on the basis of a telephone reference which the referee is unwilling to confirm in writing. This is because, should you be challenged, you have no evidence to justify the basis of your decision. If someone offers to give you a verbal reference only, you should try to establish what they would be prepared to put in writing. If they are not prepared to put anything in writing, record them as being unwilling to provide a reference and take matters up with the candidate on that basis.

Letters to applicants

Although some organisations tell applicants that if they do not get a response they can assume they have been unsuccessful, it is better practice not to leave people wondering, but to write one way or the other once you have completed shortlisting.

If you are prepared to offer feedback, either offer to provide it on request, or give a standardised comment in the letter, along the lines of 'other applicants met the person specification more precisely' or 'other applicants had more of the experience we were looking for'. You may or may not then offer to provide further information on request.

After the interviews you would be expected to write to all candidates, and again to have a policy on whether to provide or offer feedback.

The letter to the successful candidate (see Appendix G) is particularly important as you must be very careful not to find yourself committed to a contract until you are ready. You must therefore make it clear that you are offering them the job 'subject to satisfactory references', 'subject to proof of entitlement to work', 'subject to a satisfactory CRB check', 'subject to agreement on the starting salary', or whatever loose ends remain to be tied up.

How long to keep papers about unsuccessful candidates

Once you have made your decision, it is possible that the unsuccessful candidates might challenge the decision or claim discrimination. You must therefore keep all the relevant papers so that you can defend your decision and show that you acted fairly. You should keep:

- all application forms;
- all records of the shortlisting process;
- all the interview panel's notes and records.

These should all be kept securely together for six months. The time limit for a claim of discriminatory treatment is normally three months, but this can be extended. It is therefore wise to allow this amount of leeway.

After that, there is generally no good reason to keep any information about the unsuccessful candidates, and their information should be securely destroyed (see Chapter 4). (If candidates have provided a portfolio or samples of work, you may want to offer to return this material to them.)

You might want to keep some information longer than this, where similar jobs might come up in the near future and you are likely to want to ask unsuccessful applicants to reapply. In such cases you only need to keep a record of the name and a few relevant details, so the bulk of the material should still be destroyed, as above.

If you are going to retain any information, you should make sure that the people concerned know this. The best place is almost always on the application form. Since some people may not want their details kept on file for future vacancies, you should give them the opportunity to opt out of this.

Information Commissioner's benchmarks on retention of recruitment records

1   Establish and adhere to retention periods for recruitment records that are based on a clear business need.

2   Destroy information obtained by a vetting exercise as soon as possible, or in any case within 6 months. A record of the result of vetting or verification can be retained.

3   Consider carefully which information contained on an application form is to be transferred to the worker's employment record. Delete information irrelevant to on-going employment.

4   Delete information about criminal convictions collected in the course of the recruitment process once it has been verified through a Criminal Records Bureau disclosure, unless in exceptional circumstances the information is clearly relevant to the on going employment relationship.

5   Advise unsuccessful applicants that there is an intention to keep their names on file for future vacancies (if appropriate) and give them the opportunity to have their details removed from the file.

6   Ensure that personal data obtained during the recruitment process are securely stored or are destroyed.

What to transfer to the successful candidate's personnel file

When the recruitment process is complete and you have appointed a new member of staff, you need to decide what material from the recruitment process should be transferred to their personnel file.

The principles here, as always, are to do with relevance. If you might have a good reason for referring back to the information, keep it. If not, destroy it. This leads to the following possible outcome.

- Application form and any other supporting hard information or evidence provided by the applicant: keep. If it should turn out that the candidate lied, you would need the evidence to justify dismissal (but see further discussion below).
- A portfolio, samples of work or other background material: return to applicant, if they wish, or destroy.
- Verification of qualifications and professional status: keep, unless it has expired (for example where a registration has to be periodically renewed).
- Copy(ies) of approved document(s) showing entitlement to work: keep. If one is a document that is more appropriately kept with payroll material, for example, by the keep a note in the file of what document you relied on.
- References: keep. There have been cases of forged references; again the evidence would be required for dismissal.
- CRB checks: record the fact that a check was carried out and that it showed no reason to prevent appointment, and keep a note of the reference number, but destroy the results themselves unless you are required to keep these (for example by the Care Standards Commission Inspectorate).
- Equal opportunities monitoring information: destroy once the analysis has been done. If you have a policy of monitoring the composition of your workforce and want to keep this type of information, see Chapter 12.
- Interview notes and other procedural material: destroy after six months. These are no longer relevant once your decision cannot be revoked, but may be needed to prove that the appointed candidate was the best if the decision is challenged.
- Correspondence with the applicant about interview arrangements, for example, but containing no hard information: destroy.
- Copy of the letter of appointment: keep. Anything in the letter that is not conditional (indicated by 'subject to ...') will form part of your contract with them.

The suggestion above is to keep the full application form. However, you should note the Information Commissioner's benchmark, especially regarding criminal record information. Clearly in the ideal situation you would verify the information on the application form and uncover any lies before appointing the wrong person. However, in reality people have been known to slip through even a normal level of checking.

A good compromise is to design your application form so that:

- you avoid asking about criminal record or other sensitive data unless you really have to (as discussed above); and
- sensitive data which you do not have to keep in the employment record but which is only relevant to the recruitment process can easily be detached from the rest of the form and securely disposed of.

If you are carrying out a CRB check on the successful applicant, but nevertheless need to ask on the form about criminal record because it might be relevant at the shortlisting stage, the CRB check will supersede the information on the application form. The application form information should not therefore be transferred to the employment records.

If you are not required to carry out a CRB check, it might be reasonable to retain the applicant's declaration about their record (or lack of one).

Where you ask on the application form about disability or health because it is relevant to the nature of the job, it would probably be legitimate to retain this information. If the question is only about assistance they might need during the recruitment process or at the interview, the information should not be part of the application form at all. And any information about a disability that you need in order to comply with your duties under the Disability Discrimination Act 1995 (as amended) should be collected directly from the successful applicant after their appointment, as part of the preparation for them starting work.

Chapter summary

Document	Main requirements	Retention period	File location
Job advertisement	Accuracy	While the post exists	Personnel department, but not confidential
Job description	Accuracy	While current	Open access (Copy on personnel file)
Person specification	Clear criteria	While current	As job description
Other information to enquirers	Clear and concise	As advertisement	As advertisement
Application form	Relevance to specific job, and to person specification	6 months after job filled, except for successful applicant	On personnel file (confidential)
Equal opportunities monitoring form	Response optional	Until analysis complete	As application form
Shortlisting records	Related to person spec.	6 months after job filled	As application form
Interview records	Objective, fair and consistent	6 months after job filled	As application form

Document	Main requirements	Retention period	File location
Approved document showing entitlement to work	Copy, from statutory list	6 years after employment ends (sometimes longer if subject to Care Standards)	Personnel department (highly confidential)
References	In writing	6 years after employment ends	On personnel file (confidential)
CRB reference number, outcome of CRB check and other verification results	Rigorous checks	6 years after employment ends (sometimes longer if subject to Care Standards)	On personnel file (confidential)
Details of CRB checks	As required by Care Standards	6 months after employment starts, or until next Inspection (if later)	On personnel file (confidential)
Letters to unsuccessful applicants	Clear about feedback offered	6 months after job filled	Personnel department

CONTRACTS

The contract is clearly one of the most important records to keep about an employee. A contract can consist of a number of documents, all of which may impose obligations on one or both parties. Volunteers are not employees and do not get issued with contracts of employment, although you may want to make a written agreement with them (see Chapter 17 for details).

Even if the employer does not put anything in writing, a contract of service (or employment) is assumed to exist in law. It exists as soon as an offer of work is given and accepted, and may include both implied and express terms.

'Implied terms' are not normally written down anywhere as part of the contract of employment; the law automatically places duties and obligations on both sides of the employer/employee relationship.

In any employment relationship the employer must:

- stick to minimum statutory requirements;
- pay wages;
- have a duty of care for the health and safety of the employee;
- not destroy the relationship of mutual trust and confidence;
- not vary the contract unilaterally to the detriment of the employee.

The employee must:

- obey reasonable instructions;
- exercise reasonable care and skill;
- give honest and faithful service;
- respect confidentiality and copyright.

Anything that you set out in the written contract or other contractual documents contains 'express terms'. Terms in a contract can never go below the legal minimum statutory requirements.

Express terms can be oral or written, and could be in or inferred from:

- anything in the letter of appointment;
- anything in the written statement of employment particulars;
- anything in any trade union agreement with the employer;
- anything in any other agreements regarding the employment.

The 'written statement' of contractual terms and conditions

Under the Employment Rights Act 1996 the employer must give a 'written statement of employment particulars' within the first two months of employment to every employee.

A conscientious employer will give all employees a written statement within the first few days of employment. Even if a staff member is on a probationary period, a written statement must still be given. It should set out clearly the terms of the probationary period.

Since 1 October 2004 all employers regardless of size have been required to have disciplinary procedures and grievance procedures which meet statutory requirements. They must also be in the written statement or in a document given to employees at the same time as the written statement. The requirements can be found on the Acas web site (see the Resources section on page 182) in their new guidance on disciplinary and grievance procedures.

The written statement (outlined in the Employment Rights Act 1996) must include:

- the name of the employer;
- the name of the employee;
- the job title or brief description of the job;
- the starting date of employment, and whether this employment is continuous with any previous employment;
- if the job is not permanent, the period for which the employment is expected to continue or, if it is for a fixed term, the date when it is to end;
- the place of work (or an indication that work is or may be in more than one place, and the employer's address);
- the rate of pay, including any contractual overtime and bonuses;
- the pay period;
- the hours of work;
- details of holiday entitlement and holiday pay;
- details of sickness absence entitlement and sick pay arrangements;
- details of pension rights;
- the amount of notice the employee and employer must give to terminate employment;
- the disciplinary rules and disciplinary or dismissal procedures which apply to the employee;
- the description (for example job title) or name of the person to whom the employee can appeal against any disciplinary or dismissal decision, or raise a grievance;

- the appeal procedure and the grievance procedure;
- details of any relevant collective agreements.

Additional contractual terms and conditions

As well as the particulars required in the written statement, other statutory terms arise from legislation since the Employment Rights Act.

If your contract makes no mention of particular rights at all, then the statutory minimum will apply. Even if you just offer the statutory minimum it is good practice to restate it, as it is unlikely that many employees will be familiar with all their rights. Where you offer any terms or conditions that are more generous than the statutory minimum you obviously must state them. You cannot take away statutory rights, even by agreement, unless the law specifically allows that (such as with the Working Time Regulations 1998, under which people can sign an individual agreement to opt out of the 48 hour limit to the working week – but note that this opt out is under review in 2005).

Clauses arising from legislation since the Employment Rights Act are:

- provision for unpaid leave for dealing with emergencies involving dependants;
- maternity pay and leave arrangements;
- provisions for parental leave;
- provisions for adoption leave and pay, and paternity leave and pay;
- a statement of the employee's right to request flexible working;
- a statement of the right to time off for union learning representatives;
- a requirement for the employee to declare any other employment they have (so that you know that they are within the hours limit in the Working Time Directive);
- an explanation of any monitoring you may carry out, including checking on employees' use of e-mail and the internet, listening in to phone calls, or recording them, or checking up on people via closed circuit TV (see Chapter 12).
- information you want to provide in order to ensure that you comply with the Data Protection Act 1998.

There are statutory requirements in all the areas above. Details are given on the Acas and Department of Trade and Industry (DTI) web sites (see the Resources section on pages 182, 183). If you do not say anything at all you will be bound by the statutory minimum and you may find your freedom of action curtailed. (For example, if you say nothing about monitoring of employees, then you are unlikely to be able to carry it out.)

In addition, long experience suggests that other clauses should normally be put into a contract (unless you know they don't apply), either to ensure that everyone is clear about things which might otherwise be open to differing assumptions, or to protect the employer's or employee's interests. Clauses that are commonly found in employment contracts include:

- that staff inform you of any cautions or convictions they receive during their employment which may affect their suitability for that type of work (for example if their post requires an Enhanced CRB check);
- rules on what happens to extraneous remuneration (for example speaker fees paid to the employee where the invitation arises directly from their work for you);
- a provision to make deductions from pay for accidental overpayment, for loans, or to cover damages;
- any rules for reimbursement of expenses incurred in the course of the employee's work;
- provision for a normal retirement age;
- a right for you to vary the contract reasonably in cases where you are updating it according to new statutory requirements or making minor additions (but see the section below on varying the contract);
- any provision you make for compassionate leave, unpaid leave or sabbaticals;
- a requirement on the employee to comply with internal policies such as health and safety, equal opportunities, no smoking or media relations;
- a statement of the employee's duty of confidentiality regarding information about your business;
- a requirement to provide evidence of motor insurance, if relevant;
- a clear allocation of copyright for anything written by the employee in the course of their work (which normally belongs to the employer);
- a statement of the employee's right to take reasonable time off for public duties, and any provision you make to pay them for some or all of this;
- provisions for redundancy notice and pay, if these are more generous than the statutory entitlement;
- leave arrangements for same sex partners if these are more generous than statutory rights.

Information about most of the items in the list above can be found in standard employment reference books and also on government web sites, which you should check for the most up-to-date position (see the Resources section on page 181).

Data Protection clauses in contracts

There is some debate about whether you need the consent of employees to hold information about them. While some practitioners recommend that a contract should specify that the employee gives this consent, there is a case for saying that you probably do not need consent for holding anything which is not 'sensitive data' (see Chapter 3 and also Chapter 11 where health records are discussed). Some would argue that 'consent' from employees, where they have little if any choice in the matter, is not genuinely 'freely given', as required by the European Directive on which the Data Protection Act is based.

What is worth ensuring is that employees are made aware of what data you hold about them and how you use it. This would include any of the following which are not already reasonably obvious:

- any types of data you collect about them;
- any additional uses you make of their data (such as passing employee details to the events department to seek participants in sponsored events);
- any disclosure of personal information to outside bodies (such as project funders or pension companies);
- any requirement for an employee's details or photograph to appear on your web site.

You may also want to reassure staff about anything that you do *not* do with their data, or that you will only do with their consent. Where it is possible to offer a choice, you should do so. This might well apply in all the cases listed above. While it is possible to include this with the contract, it would be better practice to address it separately, as part of the induction process.

At the point where staff sign the contract, some advisers recommend that you make it explicit that the employee has read and understood the section on Data Protection, and that they consent to your use of their data. However, it is hard to see the argument for singling out the Data Protection parts of the contract statement. They should, of course, read and understand the whole document.

Drawing up a contract

Many of your contractual terms will be the same for all staff, or substantially the same, with only minor variations. (For example the rules about taking holidays will be the same, even if the amount of entitlement varies.) It is common practice to have a standard set of terms and conditions which apply to all staff, together with a letter of appointment for each individual, specifying the provisions that are particular to them.

This is perfectly acceptable, as long as everyone ends up with a clear statement of all the information which must be in the principal statement, and provided you realise that terms and conditions issued as part of the contract are subsequently binding. (See the discussion below on changing the contract.) In most cases your contractual documents should comprise specific terms and conditions which are unlikely to be changed for that employee (other than routine increases in salary, for example, or improvements to the terms and conditions).

It is quite possible to offer different types of contract for different types of staff, for example core staff on permanent terms, tutors on part-time term time contracts, and others on temporary contracts or casual contracts. If your organisation does this, it might happen that you have the same individual on more than one type of contract with you. This is perfectly legitimate, but you must contract with them separately for each type of work and keep excellent records of the start and end of each type of employment with you.

You may want to put any other detailed rules and guidance which you expect staff to follow into a staff handbook (see Chapter 14).

For more on contracts, including a model contract, see *The Voluntary Sector Legal Handbook* (the Resources section on page 184), but remember that employment law changes all the time, and you should regularly take qualified advice to ensure that the contracts you are issuing are legally valid and complete. Because of the rate of change in the law, it is worth reviewing your standard contract every year or two.

Varying the terms and conditions of the contract

Changes to terms and conditions in the contract of employment cannot be made unilaterally by the employer. One of the first issues to resolve is whether you want to change something which is part of the employee's contract or not. For example, if the job description is in the contract, then a change to the job description must be treated as a change to the terms and conditions of employment. If the job description is not in the contract because it has been expressly excluded by using a form of words such as: 'This job description is not part of the contract and can be amended from time to time as the needs of the organisation require', then it can be changed reasonably, without using the formal process for varying a contract.

However, a job description cannot be unilaterally changed out of all recognition. A claim of constructive dismissal could succeed if the change to the job description is too radical or involves detriment to the employee. Even where the changes are minor, it is clearly good practice to consult, even when this is not strictly legally necessary. If there is no amendment clause in the job description or the changes are substantial, for example as part of a restructuring, then the employee does have to be consulted.

If the change to the contract concerns terms and conditions, you have to look at the pay implications particularly carefully. Pay is deemed to be part of a contract and cannot be lowered without the employee's consent or you run the risk of a claim for constructive dismissal.

The contract can be changed:

- if the staff person concerned does not object to any changes proposed.
- if there is an express power in the contract of employment to vary it or introduce changes (but see above).
- if there is an implied right to introduce a change. It is usually possible to require employees to carry out their existing work by a different method, for example through the use of a new computer system. You may have to provide adequate training or retraining.

Even if you have an implied right to change the contract you must have a justifiable reason for making the change. You must consult with affected employees, be prepared to justify the change and listen to comments from those affected, and you must give proper notice of the implementation of the change.

If there is no implied or expressed right to amend the contract the employer must get the informed and express consent of the employees concerned. You could face a claim for constructive dismissal or breach of contract if you do not:

- consult the employee(s); and
- get their consent; and
- offer compensation for any loss sustained by the employee(s).

If it is not essential that all employees adopt the changes at the same time, then employers may decide to phase in the new terms as the new staff join the organisation. This area is very complex legally and if you are considering major contract variations or issuing replacement contracts you must consult with a specialist employment lawyer.

Obviously it is important to ensure that individually signed new contracts end up in the files for each employee. For minor changes you may use a signed statement agreeing to modifications, but these must be spelled out. It is *not* enough to have a statement saying something like 'I agree to the changes that have been circulated'.

Chapter summary

You must be clear about which aspects of your relationship with your employees are part of their employment contract. In many areas the law prescribes a minimum, but you must record accurately: elements which vary from employee to employee (such as the exact salary), areas where your provision is greater than the legal minimum, and issues covered in your contract where there is no statutory provision.

The law sets out the information that you must provide to all employees individually about their contract with you.

You must be very careful to record accurately any variations in an employee's contract during their employment.

Document	Main requirements	Retention period	File location
Letter of appointment to successful applicant	Clear about any conditions	6 years after employment ends	On personnel file
Written statement	Must cover all legal requirements	6 years after employment ends	On personnel file
Terms in staff handbooks, policy statements or collective agreements	May restate or add to legal minimum, not reduce rights	6 years after employment ends	On personnel file – may be combined with written statement
Letter varying contract	Must be explicit	6 years after employment ends	On personnel file
List of staff employed on what types of contract	Clear and accurate	6 years after employment ends	Personnel department

chapter 10

INDUCTION AND PROBATION

A good induction process is crucial if new staff are to perform well in their own jobs and for the organisation in general. Effective induction reduces the time and cost of the initial learning and settling in period, and minimises the number of early leavers.

Probation is not a substitute for a proper selection process; it is not a matter of putting people in the job to see if they will do, then throwing them out if they are unsuitable. However, even the best selection process may occasionally fail to choose the right person, and the probationary period is a formal way of ensuring that the new employee is given a fair chance, while protecting the organisation at the same time. It also provides the post-holder with an opportunity to explore their new post in formal review meetings and to raise issues and concerns they might have about the match between themselves, their skills and the post and skills required.

Induction

Induction should be a planned and systematic process, with record-keeping built in. This could be as simple as a checklist which forms part of the personnel record, indicating when the new employee completed each part of the process. This record can be a useful management tool, to ensure that you don't miss anything important. It is also worth keeping to support the organisation should the staff member subsequently claim that they made a mistake or performed their job poorly because they had not been properly inducted.

This means, however, that the organisation should stick to its plan if it makes one; the staff member could argue they were unsupported if the planned meetings did not take place or took place hurriedly.

There is, of course, much more to induction than the running of a formal induction course. Tuning people into the style of the organisation and ensuring that they understand its aims and values is a longer-term process, which cannot be achieved by simply going through a course. However, by the end of the induction process the new member of staff should have:

- a clear understanding of their own role and responsibilities and those of their team;
- a clear understanding of the objectives of their section or programme and their department, and how their role will help achieve these;
- familiarity with the organisation's vision, mission, values, and goals;
- an understanding of the context in which the organisation works and the methods and approaches taken;
- familiarity with the systems, policies and procedures in place at work, and understanding of their individual responsibilities for things outside their immediate job, such as health and safety or confidentiality;
- familiarity with all the practical arrangements, such as for pay, leave, time-recording, photocopying, IT systems and emergency procedures;
- successfully completed any necessary training, such as health and safety, hygiene or manual handling;
- a clear agreement with their line manager about how the working relationship will continue, including processes for support, supervision, review and development.

If staff have to attend and pass specific training before they are able to do the job, this obviously needs recording and checking very carefully.

Induction is needed not only for those new to an organisation, but also those moving to different posts. Obviously they don't need the full induction programme, but they do need help with settling into their new job or department.

Certain aspects of the induction programme, particularly in relation to safety, office layout, use of equipment, confidentiality and the main tasks of the job, will also be required for temporary, agency and any freelance staff using your premises from time to time.

The induction needs to be well planned, but flexible enough to meet the needs of the individual. The aim is to cover all the ground in the shortest effective time, but bearing in mind that a new member of staff can take in only a limited amount at a time. Too intensive a programme is likely to be ineffective. The initial few days are often detailed and quite highly structured, while the whole programme might last considerably longer – weeks or even months. Recording what has been done when is particularly important as time goes on and the induction activities start to be fitted around actual work commitments. A sample induction programme record sheet is given in Appendix I.

The induction plan should be kept in the personnel file, so that the personnel department knows what is expected to happen. In many cases it makes sense for a copy to be kept by the staff member themselves or their line manager while induction is going on, so that it can be regularly updated. The personnel file copy should be updated at key stages and both copies should be kept at least until the staff member's first supervision session, at which point it should be reviewed and arrangements made to fill any outstanding gaps. Once it is mutually agreed that all outstanding matters have been dealt with, this can be noted in the supervision record. The file copy of the induction record should be retained until six months after the end of the person's employment with you.

Probation

An unsuccessful probationary period can lead to someone losing their job, and to considerable disruption for the organisation, along with the additional cost of re-filling the post. For these reasons it is particularly important to have a proper record. If a probationary period is relatively short, the record may be combined with the induction record. Where a separate record is kept, this should normally be kept in the personnel file, so that the personnel department can monitor progress and remind the line manager, if necessary, about action that needs to be taken.

The probationary period must be for a specified time, with a clearly defined set of goals by which the new staff member's performance will be assessed. The probationary period record must set out the following.

- Goals which have been set by the organisation, but understood and agreed by the staff member. The record should be signed by the staff member to indicate their agreement.
- A clear statement of any measurable targets which the staff member is expected to meet.
- A date or dates at which progress is to be reviewed.
- A record of the outcome of each review. If it is satisfactory, the record need say nothing more; if it is not, then it should include any revised targets and a new review date, again signed by the staff member to indicate that they have understood and agreed.

If the probationary period is – in exceptional circumstances – extended, the decision and the reasons for it should be recorded and kept in the file.

If the new staff member does not pass the probationary period, don't forget that you must still follow the statutory dismissal procedure. More information on this is available from Acas (see the Resources section on page 182).

Once it is mutually agreed that the probationary period has been satisfactorily completed, a letter should be sent to the employee confirming them in post. A copy of this letter should be kept on file. The probation record should be the first entry in the employee's supervision and appraisal record, and any training needs or other issues it identifies should be referred to in the first appraisal meeting. The probation record itself should be kept until six years after the end of the person's employment with you.

Chapter summary

Your records of induction, and of a new employee's probationary period, must record their progress, and identify any issues, clearly and accurately so that you can rely on them if any question arises in future.

Document	Main requirements	Retention period	File location
Document	Main requirements	Retention period	File location
Induction record	Specific actions, kept up-to-date	Until 6 months after employment ends	Employee or line manager, copied to personnel file
Probation record	Specific goals and dates	Until 6 years after employment ends	Personnel file
Letter extending probationary period	Specific and clear	Until 6 years after employment ends	Personnel file
Letter of confirmation in post	Contractual	Until 6 years after employment ends	Personnel file

chapter 11

HOLIDAYS, SICKNESS ABSENCE AND HEALTH RECORDS

People can be away from work for many reasons, including:

- holidays (including bank holidays);
- sickness absence;
- absence connected with family or personal responsibilities, including maternity leave, paternity leave, adoption leave, time off to care for dependants or compassionate leave;
- specific reasons such as time off for public duties;
- days taken as TOIL – that is, where people work extra hours and then get the equivalent time off instead of being paid extra;
- study leave or extended unpaid leave (sometimes called a sabbatical, which is usually for a period of months, unpaid, and available after a certain length of service).

These fall into two main categories: pre-planned events – such as holidays – where employees must get approval in advance (or in other cases, such as maternity leave, must give proper notice), and unplanned events – such as sickness – where people must account for the absence after the event.

It is important to keep good records of all time off, both pre-arranged and unplanned, for the following reasons.

- You have a legal duty to give people certain time off, and must be able to show that you have met your obligations.
- The limits on the amount of work set by the Working Time Directive are based on actual time worked.
- You must know when people are planning not to be at work, so that you can manage your staff team properly and ensure that all the work is covered.
- There are likely to be pay implications. You might allow unpaid leave in certain cases. Your sickness absence policy will almost certainly specify a limit on how many days of absence will be paid, and at what rate. Maternity leave also attracts a complex range of payments over different time periods.

- You may need to know how much sickness absence each individual and your staff as a whole are taking, to ensure that you take any necessary action. If people are off sick more than you would expect, perhaps their work is making them ill, or perhaps they are taking you for a ride.

It should be an absolute rule that any time off other than for unexpected illness or emergencies must be authorised in advance, and for all leave and absence there should be a set procedure for notification and specific documentation. This makes the process fair and transparent to all staff – so that no one appears to get favourable treatment – and makes the administration considerably easier.

Much of the information about time off should be confidential. When someone is planning to be away, or when they have not turned up for work, this obviously cannot be hidden from colleagues whose work it will affect. You must have a system for ensuring that essential work is covered, that meetings and other commitments can be rearranged if necessary, and that those on reception duties can give callers accurate information. However, you must do this without unnecessarily infringing the privacy of the individual concerned. If they choose to share the reason with colleagues, that is fine, but if they do not, you should ensure that their preferences are respected.

Your systems, therefore, should distinguish between the personnel aspects of time off (kept confidential unless you have the individual's permission) and the work planning aspects (where some information must be made widely available).

Work planning around time off

The annual holiday and absence chart is a familiar sight on many office walls, and can be an effective tool if it is kept fully up-to-date. However, in order to preserve confidentiality there should normally only be three categories of entry:

- planned time off;
- emergency absence from work;
- time away from the office, working elsewhere.

Only in the final category should any further information normally be shown (for example if someone is working at home and may be contacted, or at a conference and therefore not available at all).

Similar principles apply to the office diary. Everyone is entitled to know whether their colleagues are available, both at the time, to avoid wasted effort trying to track them down, and for the future so that meetings and other events can be planned. It is therefore perfectly acceptable for the organisation to insist that its staff record their comings and goings during the day as well as future commitments. Indeed, much of the benefit of an in/out board or a consolidated diary (whether it is kept on paper or electronically) is lost if even a few people fail to enter their movements.

Where someone is away from the office but working, the diary can record where they are and any options for contacting them. If they are not working, for whatever reason, the diary need only record that the person is off and therefore unavailable.

One of the benefits of an accurate chart or diary is that a person's colleagues and contacts can be given information about when they will be available again. Sometimes, however, this might not be known, and the reason may be a delicate issue such as illness of the individual or a close relative, or even suspension for disciplinary reasons. In order to avoid ill-informed speculation it may be worth obtaining the staff member's permission to inform their colleagues of the situation (or in extreme cases to decide to inform them without permission). Where this happens, however, particular care must be taken to restrict the information to those who need to know and prevent it going further. Anyone carrying out reception duties, and anyone dealing with the absent person's calls, post or e-mail, should be given clear instructions to say only that the colleague is away.

Individual records of time off

The personnel department, and almost always the staff member's line manager, need to know much more about leave and absence than other colleagues.

The information kept in the individual personnel records must show:

- exactly when the staff member was away;
- why they were away;
- whether the time off was paid or unpaid (remembering that there may be a limit on how much time off for a given reason is paid, and at what rate, after which pay is reduced or stops altogether);
- evidence of whether leave was authorised in advance;
- evidence of whether absence was justified, if not authorised in advance (such as a medical certificate or self-certificate);
- evidence that the correct procedures were followed;
- any action taken as a result of absence (such as return-to-work interviews or a referral for medical assessments).

Your forms on which leave or absence can be authorised must record all the information listed above. It is possible to use just one form, both for pre-planned leave and unplanned absence, although many organisations have two separate ones. Appendix J shows the two-form approach.

As well as keeping records on each individual instance, it is useful to keep a summary (see sample in Appendix J) showing all absence and time off by each employee in the course of a year, and the reason for it. This will help in practical ways, if there is any question over the amount of remaining holiday allowance, for example, and also for performance monitoring, if there is any suggestion that the pattern of absence should be investigated. Although it would, in theory, be possible to recreate the summary from the individual records of events, it makes sense to keep any summary sheets for at least as long as the underlying evidence, in case any disagreement arises – for example about how much holiday or TOIL should have been carried forward. You may even want to keep the summary sheets for comparison with future years, after the detailed records have been destroyed.

Many leave and absence records can, of course, be held electronically, but you are likely still to need paper records such as signed absence authorisations and medical certificates.

If you compile statistics on absence there is no restriction on publishing them, provided you are careful not to enable people to identify any individual. For example, if you want to compare the rate of absence in different departments, it would not be acceptable to include the figures for departments with just one or two people in them. Their figures should be amalgamated with others before the data is made public.

Sharing summarised absence records of teams or departments with the senior management team is a different matter. There may very well be a need to discuss these in order to decide on any management action that might be needed, but it will rarely be necessary to disclose detailed reasons for individual absence.

In other circumstances it may be appropriate to discuss the absence record of a particular individual with a senior line manager.

Information Commissioner's benchmarks on sickness and absence records

1   Keep sickness and accident records separately from absence records. Do not use sickness or accident records for a particular purpose when records of absence could be used instead.

2   Ensure that the holding and use of sickness and accident records satisfies a sensitive data condition.

3   Only disclose information from sickness or accident records about a worker's illness, medical condition or injury where there is a legal obligation to do so, where it is necessary for legal proceedings or where the worker has given explicit consent to the disclosure.

4   Do not make the sickness, accident or absence records of individual workers available to other workers, other than to provide managers with information about those who work for them in so far as this is necessary for them to carry out their managerial roles.

Health information: general considerations

Absence for health reasons, and any other record relating to a person's health, raises particular issues, because any information about a person's health is considered to be 'sensitive' data under the Data Protection Act 1998. The Information Commissioner's Code of Practice Part 4, published in December 2004, sets out some basic principles, but is unhelpfully vague about a key area of uncertainty: whether there are any circumstances in which an employer can hold or use health information without having either the individual's consent or a legal obligation.

The rules apply to any health information you acquire. This could include, for example:

■   information about someone's previous health obtained during the recruitment process;
■   information provided by an employee in relation to absence for health reasons;
■   information supplied at the employer's request by an external doctor or occupational health service;
■   information about a person's disabilities that you need to have because of your Disability Discrimination Act 1995 duties;
■   records of accidents or injuries at work.

Although there may occasionally be information about health which does not count as 'personal data' because it is held in manual files which are not a 'relevant filing system' (see Chapter 3), you should treat all information about health matters as confidential. The only practical difference would arise in relation to the individual's right of access to the data you hold.

The Information Commissioner points out that people generally have legitimate expectations of privacy and are likely to find questions about their health intrusive. Information should therefore only be collected or kept if there is a clear justification for it, and your staff should be fully informed about what kind of health information you hold.

You should also look for less intrusive alternatives. For example, in order to make effective and fair decisions about a person's fitness for work you are expected to get advice from a qualified health professional, not to make your own assumptions. Whether you are relying on the staff member's own doctor to make that judgement or on someone appointed by you, such as an occupational health service, you really only need to know their recommendation, not the full health details on which they have based their decision. It would therefore be unacceptable to ask for, or keep, the specific details.

That still leaves the question of how you can meet one of the Conditions set out in Schedule 3 of the Data Protection Act for holding 'sensitive' data. In routine situations it is hard to see how any of the Conditions other than the first two might apply. These are:

1. *The data subject has given his explicit consent to the processing of the personal data.'*
2. *The processing is necessary for the purposes of exercising or performing any right or obligation which is conferred or imposed by law on the data controller in connection with employment.'*

You should note that, like all legislation, the Data Protection Act is not written in gender-neutral terms, but references to 'he' also mean 'she', and so on.

The Information Commissioner suggests that an employer may find difficulty relying on consent, since they have an unfair bargaining advantage: 'we won't give you the job if you don't agree'. Obviously, there are cases where it is appropriate to ask for consent. For example, you may have a reason for collecting information about someone's health but could cope without it, or you may want to use health information in a particular way – for example by disclosing it to other staff – but again don't need to insist. In these cases, if you don't get consent, you don't record the information or don't use it in that particular way.

There are relatively few cases where there is a legal obligation to hold health information. Obvious examples include records kept for Statutory Sick Pay (SSP) or Statutory Maternity Pay (SMP) purposes, information relating to Health and Safety or reportable accidents, or information needed in order to comply with the Disability Discrimination Act.

Do employers have a 'right ... conferred by law' to hold information for reasons such as personnel management or work planning? The Information Commissioner gives no specific examples where this would be the case. Nor, however, does the Code indicate what other Schedule 3 Condition might be met. Nevertheless, it goes on to recommend good practice in a number of areas where it is undoubtedly at the employer's discretion whether to obtain and use information about health.

This chapter therefore assumes that employers have a legitimate reason for holding a variety of health information about their staff, beyond that required by law, and that this is compatible with the Data Protection Act. The fact that health information is 'sensitive' does mean, however, that particular care must be taken.

Two other Conditions should be mentioned. These would not normally be relevant, but might apply in specific cases. The third Condition is about preventing harm. It permits processing without consent where:

> '3. *The processing is necessary-*
> (a) *in order to protect the vital interests of the data subject or another person, in a case where-*
> (i) *consent cannot be given by or on behalf of the data subject, or*
> (ii) *the data controller cannot reasonably be expected to obtain the consent of the data subject, or*
> (b) *in order to protect the vital interests of another person, in a case where consent by or on behalf of the data subject has been unreasonably withheld.'*

This could be used to disclose health information in an emergency, for example, or to protect clients from exposure to dangerous illnesses where an employee was unreasonably reluctant to allow their condition to be taken into account.

The other Condition is the eighth, which permits processing without consent where:

> '8. (1) *The processing is necessary for medical purposes and is undertaken by-*
> (a) *a health professional, or*
> (b) *a person who in the circumstances owes a duty of confidentiality which is equivalent to that which would arise if that person were a health professional.*
> (2) *In this paragraph 'medical purposes' includes the purposes of preventative medicine, medical diagnosis, medical research, the provision of care and treatment and the management of healthcare services.'*

Note that this only allows the information to be held by a health professional, and only for medical purposes, such as diagnosis, care and treatment. It would not apply to information held by an employer for management purposes or as part of an absence control procedure.

Disability information

Clearly the second Schedule 3 Condition (discussed above) allows you to hold information about the disability of any employee or job applicant which you might need in order to comply with your responsibility to make 'reasonable adjustments' under the Disability Discrimination Act (this Act has been substantially amended since 1995 and further amendments are planned). These adjustments might include changes to their hours of work, to your working practices, or to the physical arrangement of your premises, for example.

We are not concerned here with an employer's general responsibility to avoid discrimination on grounds of disability, but with information about a particular individual relating to their specific needs.

A useful Code of Practice is published on-line by the Disability Rights Commission (see the Resources section on page 186). This suggests that it is certainly good practice for an employer to seek information about disability, and to make it easy for employees or applicants to make their needs known:

> '... the employer only has a duty to make an adjustment if it knows, or could reasonably be expected to know, that the employee has a disability and is likely to be placed at a substantial disadvantage. The employer must, however, do all it can reasonably be expected to do to find out whether this is the case.'

You should therefore encourage people, especially during your recruitment procedure and your induction procedure, to inform you about their needs. You may want to put a specific invitation on your application form for people to discuss any adjustments they might need, but you should not have a blanket question asking about disability: unless the disability relates to their capacity to do the job the information would be excessive.

In order to make sure that this information is collected consistently and sensitively, it is best for this to be the responsibility of the personnel department. However, you also need to make other members of staff aware that if a disability need comes to their attention they *must* pass the information on to the personnel department for further action. The Disability Rights Commission Code of Practice says this explicitly:

> 'If an employer's agent or employee (such as an occupational health adviser, a personnel officer or line manager or recruitment agent) knows, in that capacity, of an employee's disability, the employer will not usually be able to claim that it does not know of the disability, and that it therefore has no obligation to make a reasonable adjustment.'

Information should, of course, be obtained directly from the individual as far as possible, so that you can be sure it is relevant and accurate. You should record in their personnel file the information they give you and any action you agree to take. If you agree periodic reviews they should also be documented in the file.

If people do not tell you about any disability-related need, then you do not have to make any adjustments. However, you must remember that it is still possible to break the law by discriminating against disabled people in general, even if you don't know that a particular person has a disability.

What if someone asks me to keep their disability a secret?

Disability information is 'sensitive' in Data Protection terms. You must, therefore, ensure that it is kept strictly confidential only to those people who genuinely need to know it. You should always take into account the views of the data subject on how the information should be used, and get their consent where possible, but you may have no choice. Two cases will serve as examples:

■ where the 'reasonable adjustment' you need to make will reveal widely that the person is being treated differently; or

■ where the individual asks their line manager, for example, to keep their knowledge of the disability secret and not pass it on to the personnel department.

In the first case, you are constrained by the fact that people cannot give up their rights under the Disability Discrimination Act, even if they want to. There may be scope for negotiating with the individual to make the adjustment as inconspicuous as possible, but in the end the adjustment must be made.

In the second case, by telling the line manager the individual has informed an 'agent' of the employer. The employer therefore must act on the information, so the line manager may have no choice about passing the information on if an adjustment needs to be made. They should, of course, reassure the individual about the confidential status of the information. Even if the line manager and the individual agree that no adjustment needs to be made, failing to record the disability formally could leave the employer open to a claim in future if the disability becomes worse and starts to affect the employee's performance.

Medical reports

You may occasionally want to obtain a medical report about an employee, for example where you are not satisfied with their stated reasons for absence on health grounds, to check the progress of their recovery from illness, or to check their fitness for a particular task or role.

If the report is not related in any way to treatment of the individual, they have no right to see the report. So, for example, you might commission a report from a specialist purely to give their opinion on the employee's – or job applicant's – current state of health or fitness, and this could legitimately be withheld from the employee. (Note, however, that if you want to be able to insist on employees being medically examined you should make provision for this in the contract.)

You also have the option of requesting a report from the employee's or job applicant's own doctor, or any medical practitioner who has been involved in treating them. This is covered by the Access to Medical Reports Act 1988, and the employee, or prospective employee, has specific rights, including:

- to refuse consent for the employer to be supplied with a medical report, or even for the employer to ask for one;
- to have access to the report before it is supplied to the employer;
- to ask the doctor to change the report before supplying it, and to attach their own views if the doctor refuses.

The employer must tell people about their rights, and must get their consent before applying for a medical report from a doctor who has been treating them. It is strongly recommended to get this consent in writing, as you may have to prove to the medical practitioner that you have obtained consent.

The doctor must keep the report for six months, during which time the individual has the right to inspect it further. The procedure for individual access is laid down. The employer must tell the individual that the report has been requested. The individual must then contact the medical practitioner within 21 days to make arrangements to see the report. The individual does not have a right to a copy of the report, although it is common practice for a copy to be provided.

When you receive a medical report you should, of course, keep it strictly confidential, and only allow access by people who need to be involved in making any decision. Once the need for the report has passed, you do not need to keep either the report itself (which should be securely destroyed) or the consent form. You may want to keep a record of the outcome: for instance, that a report was commissioned and concluded that the employee was fit for work.

The employee also has the right, under the Data Protection Act, to apply for access to their own medical records. The employer, however, is forbidden from making use of this as a back door means of access. The Data Protection Act expressly outlaws any contractual provision which tries to force anyone to get access to their own medical records and show them to, or provide a copy to, the employer.

The result is, therefore, that you cannot get a report from the employee's own doctor if the employee doesn't want you to, and you can only insist on them going for a medical (from a doctor you commission, or from the occupational health service, for example) if your contract allows you to.

Sickness absence procedures

Normally you will insist that employees notify you as soon as possible if they are absent because of illness, so that you can make any necessary arrangements to cover their work. Prompt notice is especially important if they are on a shift which needs a fixed number of people to be present. Some employers specify that they expect the employee to make contact in person, where this is possible, which at least gives the opportunity to ask them if there is any particular piece of work which someone else will need to handle, and may discourage malingering. It is usual to require the employee to give a reason. It is also usual to expect them to keep you updated on how they are doing, and how long they expect to be away. A requirement for employees to follow health absence procedures is usually put into the contract.

You should specify the appropriate mechanism for staff to contact you about absence, and not leave it to chance.

- The ideal person to receive the absence notification is the employee's line manager, since they can legitimately ask the reason for the absence, and can also check with the employee whether there is any specific work that needs to be covered or rearranged.
- Where it is not possible for the individual to contact their line manager, the next best contact is the personnel department. While they will not be as much use in rearranging work, at least they will be able to record the absence and the reason, and pass the information on to the line manager.
- If neither of these two options is available, the employee should leave a message with reception, or with a colleague, but only to say that they are unable to come to work. The reasons, and any other aspect of the absence, can be followed up later by the line manager or personnel department, and it should be made clear to all staff that they are not expected to ask about the reason for absence if they take such a message.

Even where people contact their line manager in the first instance, the absence records should be kept by the personnel department. In a typical procedure this would include:

- a formal record of the absence notification, signed by the person who was notified, and recording the date and time that notification was made.

- a self-certificate completed by the employee when they return to work, in the case of absences of up to seven days, or certificate(s) from a medical practitioner, confirming the reason for absence.
- an absence form completed by the employee when they return to work.
- a record of the outcome of any return to work interview.

The individual's line manager will normally be responsible for carrying out any necessary procedures and ensuring that the relevant forms are completed. The personnel department, however, should oversee the process and chase up any late or missing documents.

Sickness absence is also tied up with SSP (see the Resources section on page 188). Under the SSP Regulations, at the time of writing, a certificate showing the reasons for absence is normally required for any absence of four or more days. For periods up to seven days the employee can write their own certificate (a 'self-certificate'); longer than that and the certificate must come from a doctor. Some employers have their own rules which require a self-certificate for all sickness absence, even shorter than four days.

The personnel department (not the line manager) should liaise with payroll. Payroll needs an accurate record of the sickness absence – and in most cases will need to know whether any particular period of absence is related to a previous absence (since a series of absences for the same reason are usually treated as one incident in calculating when someone has used up their entitlement to sick pay). Payroll will also need to calculate the financial side of SSP. (For example, some of the money paid out by the employer under SSP can be reclaimed if the total SSP costs in any one month are more than 13% of the total Class 1 National Insurance.) For details of how to operate SSP, and sample forms to use (including self-certification forms) see the Inland Revenue web site in the Resources section (page 188).

You may reasonably ask employees to arrange any dental or medical appointments outside working hours, while recognising that this is not always possible. Where employees take time off for appointments during working hours you may ask them to use some of any TOIL (time off in lieu) that they are owed. Otherwise, the absence should be authorised in the normal way, and you may reasonably ask for evidence of the appointment (such as a letter from the hospital or an appointment card).

Absence management

You may feel that excessive absenteeism is costly and you want to have procedures to manage or control absence. Proper procedures for reporting sickness, for applying for leave, and for recording absence are all part of this. If people do not follow the procedures you would be justified in taking action, provided you have made the rules clear and the procedures appropriate.

Return to work interviews, where absence has not been authorised in advance, are another common feature of absence management. If you operate a policy of return to work interviews, these must on a fair basis: following all absences of a certain length of time, or if the employee's pattern of absence has already been raised as a cause for concern, for example. Your interview should review the absence report submitted by the employee, and you should record, in summarised form:

- any concerns you raise (such as pointing out a pattern of absence, or checking that they are really fit to return to work);
- the employee's response;
- any action you propose to take, such as a further review after a specified period, or referral to Occupational Health.

This record should be prepared as soon as possible after the interview, and the employee should be asked to sign a copy to show that they agree that it is an accurate record (even if they are not in full agreement with your actions). One copy should be provided to the employee and the copy they have signed should be kept in their file.

It is important that you do not discriminate unfairly against an employee with a poor attendance record caused by a disability. This is not always as straightforward as it sounds, because, for example, a variety of mental conditions and illnesses which may not be obvious, are classed by law as disabilities. You must, therefore, be sure that when conducting return to work interviews you have access to records of any disability you have been made aware of, and that your investigation gives the employee the opportunity to make you aware of any disability that might have contributed to the absence.

Health and safety, accidents and occupational health

There are strict rules about the reporting of serious accidents and other events which might affect people's health. These are set out in the Reporting of Injuries, Diseases and Dangerous Occurrences Regulations 1995 (RIDDOR). At the same time, it is important to keep track of any incident in order to manage the health and safety of your personnel and ensure that avoidable problems do not recur.

Since the relevant records often involve the health or medical condition of those involved, the Data Protection rules on 'sensitive' data must be observed.

The Health and Safety Executive (HSE) has produced a new style of accident book which is compliant with Data Protection (see the Resources section on page 188). This is designed to enable the book to remain accessible yet at the same time keeping the information confidential. The details of each incident are entered on a separate sheet which is removed from the book and stored securely. These sheets, along with any other reports of a similar nature, should be kept together in one place, to make their audit and analysis more convenient. At the same time, if an employee has been involved in an incident, this should be recorded in their file, with a copy of (or reference to) the full details so that any consequent problems can be followed through.

The HSE accident book gives further information on when you must make a report to the HSE or your local authority, under RIDDOR. In particular, any injury which is not serious enough to be reported immediately, but which results in more than three days' absence, must be reported within ten days. You must, therefore, not just record the incident as soon as it occurs and decide whether to report it, but also keep track of how long any resulting absence lasts in case a later report is required.

The accident records themselves (and the cover of the accident book when all the forms in it have been used) must be kept for at least three years. (The book itself contains instructions for how it should be used.) The information in the individual personnel record should also be kept for at least three years.

Because some accidents and occupational health problems may have long term repercussions, the details of these should be kept, in effect, permanently, even after the staff member has left. Medical records under the Control of Asbestos at Work Regulations, for example, must be kept for 40 years from the date of the last entry.

Maternity and other family-related leave

Maternity absence is subject to complex statutory rules on the minimum amount of leave which must be offered, the time limits within which it may be taken, and the amount of pay or Statutory Maternity Pay (SMP) which is due (see the Resources section on pages 188–9). In order not to make a mistake, it is particularly important, therefore, to keep very careful records. You may want to consider using a specific maternity leave record sheet such as that shown in Appendix J (which could usefully be handled by a spreadsheet to calculate many of the key dates automatically for you).

Maternity leave records should be held by the personnel department, while the financial side of SMP and arrangements for any period of unpaid leave should, of course, be handled by payroll (see Chapter 5). The personnel department must take care to give payroll very clear information at all times, in order for the correct payments to be made. The Inland Revenue web site has a useful SMP calculator and other information (see the Resources section on page 188).

In addition to maternity leave and pay, which have been available for some time, employees now also have rights to:

- paid leave for adoptive parents and for paternity leave,
- unpaid parental leave and time off to care for dependants; and
- the right for parents of children up to the age of six, or disabled children up to the age of 18, to apply to work flexibly.

For all of these the employee has to meet certain requirements (they only get parental leave if they have legal responsibility for the child, for example) and for all except time off to care for dependants the employee has to have a given length of service. It is important to familiarise yourself with the regulations, and you must keep good records of any application for statutory leave and your response. (See also the discussion below on holidays and other time off.)

If your contract provides better conditions than the statutory entitlement, your records should obviously be based on the contractual provision.

Holidays and other time off

Employees have statutory rights to time off for many different reasons (see Appendix K); workers have very limited statutory rights (see Appendix B). These are non-negotiable, although in some cases people do not qualify until they have worked with you for a certain time, or they only qualify if they fall into a certain category.

You may offer additional rights in a contract, such as more holiday than the statutory minimum, additional sick leave or compassionate leave. The contract may specify additional qualification periods and reporting requirements.

A further complication is that in some cases the amount of time off an employee is entitled to (or the minimum) is fixed in law, while in others the law provides that you must allow 'reasonable' amounts, or gives the employer a certain amount of discretion. Allowing no leave at all, or allowing leave to some employees but not others for no good reason, could be found to be 'unreasonable'.

All this means that you must be very clear, in relation to each individual employee or worker, how much time off they are entitled to for all the various reasons and how much they have already had in this year (or whatever period you work to).

We have already considered the two main cases where you have no effective control over timing: sickness absence and maternity and other family-related leave. Here we look at time off which is normally pre-arranged, and where you may have some leeway over *when* it can be taken. These include, for example:

■ holidays;
■ time off for trade union and public duties;
■ compassionate or bereavement leave;
■ sabbaticals (where someone takes an extended period of leave after a certain number of years' service).

Whatever the basis of the leave, you need to ensure that it is planned, and that staff members give you the amount of notice required by law or in your contract. Your record-keeping must be able to show whether people have had the time off they are entitled to and also that they have been treated fairly. This means that you must record:

■ the request for leave or time off;
■ your response – whether the leave was granted or not, and on what terms, including whether paid or unpaid;
■ the leave that was actually taken.

You should insist that any request for time off is normally made in writing, a reasonable time in advance, using a standard form. Using a standard form ensures that all the information you need about dates and authorisation is recorded unambiguously. (See the sample form in Appendix J.) Where someone takes time off in an emergency (for example a bereavement) you should, of course, be reasonably flexible: you could receive the request and agree the leave by phone, but complete the form on the employee's return.

In many cases the employee will have requested the time off informally in advance, and you will have no difficulty agreeing to it. For this situation your form can just record that the application for leave was agreed. Where you turn down someone's request, however, you must do more. You must be able to show a reasonable and legally-allowable justification for the refusal, which is fair to the individual.

For example, if the statutory entitlement is to 'reasonable' amounts of time off, you may need access not only to a full and accurate record of that employee's time off for the same reason in the recent past, but also to records of the amount of time other employees have had off for the same reason. In deciding whether to grant a request for time off you should refer to this information, and you should use it (and any provisions in your contract) as evidence if you turn the application down.

With holidays you may have to be able to show that you have treated all your staff on an equal basis. Continually refusing the same person holiday at popular times might amount to discrimination; so might giving one person holiday at short notice but insisting that another applies a long time in advance.

In making your response it is also essential that everyone is clear from the outset whether the leave is paid or not, and that relevant information about unpaid leave gets passed on for payroll purposes.

Finally, don't forget to record the actual days away in the employee's record, not the planned leave shown on the application. It could be, for all sorts of reasons, that events don't turn out as planned.

Access to e-mails when staff are away

You have to be careful if you ever want to read people's e-mails. In most circumstances it is illegal to intercept – which means to monitor to or to record – any electronic communication such as a phone call, or an e-mail, during its transmission, because of the Regulation of Investigatory Powers Act 2000.

However, you are permitted to intercept communications if you meet the conditions set out in the Lawful Business Practice Regulations. In brief, the conditions are that interception must be properly authorised, for permitted purposes only; 'reasonable' efforts must be made to inform callers about the interception; and you must respect people's right to confidentiality, which may mean that you should have their consent to the interception.

Where you are accessing e-mails after transmission (that is, when it is in the Inbox or Sent Items, for example) then it is not unlawful under the Regulation of Investigatory Powers Act 2000. However, you must still comply with the Data Protection Act 1998 and take account of the individual's right to confidentiality.

What this means in practice is as follows.

- You must tell your staff the circumstances in which you might access their e-mails in their absence – for example in your staff handbook, or in a separate Acceptable Use Policy (AUP) for computers and the internet.
- Where time off is pre-arranged you should, if possible, make suitable arrangements for incoming e-mails to be forwarded to someone else, so that you do not need to access the absent employee's whole set of e-mails.

- If you do need access it must be properly authorised; the person who needs access must make the case, and an appropriately senior person must agree.
- You must have a good business reason for accessing the e-mails – for example if you need to pass their work over to someone else for the duration of their absence and you need to check the latest contact they have had with people outside your organisation.
- You should not access e-mails where the absence is expected to be short term and there is no necessity to deal with any issues before the employee's expected return.
- If you allow people to make any private use of your e-mail system you must tell them how to keep their private e-mails separate from work ones (for example by putting them in a separate folder), so that you can access their work e-mails without infringing their privacy.

Chapter summary

It is important to keep full and accurate records of all employee time off, both pre-arranged and unplanned. These must show the amount of time off and the reason, as well as clear evidence that the time off was legitimate.

It is common to have separate procedures for requesting and authorising planned time off and for justifying unplanned absence. These should specify what type of authorisation or evidence is appropriate for which type and amount of time off.

There are legal provisions for much time off, including minimum amounts which must be provided.

Recording systems must also provide information necessary for adjusting pay, where this is affected by time off.

Much of the information about time off and the reasons for it should be strictly confidential. Procedures for reporting absence and for work planning around people's time off should be designed with confidentiality in mind.

Health information is 'sensitive' under the Data Protection Act, and should be used in compliance with the Information Commissioner's Code of Practice.

Information on an individual's disability is covered by a Code of Practice from the Disability Rights Commission.

Employee consent is required if a medical report is to be provided by their own doctor.

There are statutory reporting requirements for accidents and some other incidents.

Access to employees' e-mails during transmission must comply with the Lawful Business Practice Regulations.

Document	Main requirements	Retention period	File location
Summary(ies) of leave and absence	Accuracy	Until 6 years after employment ends	Personnel file
Absence and leave charts or diaries	Not to reveal confidential information	While current	Within relevant team
Authorisation for leave, or requests that have been denied	Contain all relevant information	Until 6 years after employment ends	Personnel file
Self-certificates and medical certificates	Clarity	Until 6 years after employment ends	Personnel file (confidential)
Records of SSP, SMP, etc.	Accuracy	3 years after the end of the tax year they relate to	Payroll (or personnel file)
Information on an employee's disability	Employee consent, because 'sensitive'	Until 6 months after employment ends	Personnel file (confidential)
Medical reports	Employee consent if from own doctor	Until 6 months after employment ends	Personnel file (confidential)
Medical reports relating to specific hazards	Comply with legal requirements	Up to 40 or more years, depending on specific regulations	Personnel file
Accident books and accident records	Comply with legal reporting requirements	3 years after date of last entry	Personnel department
Individual records of accidents, etc.	Appropriate detail	3 years after accident	Personnel file

chapter 12

PERFORMANCE RECORDS AND MONITORING

In addition to all your practical records about people's pay, contact details, absence and so on, it is quite likely that you will want to take some steps to ensure that they are doing their job as effectively as possible. These steps might include:

- a system of regular supervision sessions;
- an appraisal programme;
- training, on the job or through courses;
- timesheets or a system of clocking in and out;
- monitoring employees' internet access;
- security and CCTV systems.

For those times in the employment relationship when things just aren't going right you must, by law, have a proper disciplinary procedure, a proper grievance procedure and a proper appeal procedure. All these procedures must meet the statutory requirements.

All these systems and procedures generate records which you may have to depend on in taking serious action, possibly even dismissal. As in so many other areas, the quality of your records is crucial.

Recording performance management meetings with individual staff

Performance management should be seen by staff as supportive and constructive. This is not always the case however: your line managers may not handle it as well as they should or, where you are taking disciplinary action, the individual is almost bound to feel unhappy. This makes it doubly important for your records of the contact you have with staff and the action you are taking to be as accurate and uncontroversial as possible.

In most cases you should ensure that the *record* of what has happened is agreed by all sides to be accurate, even if the outcome of a meeting or the action you propose to take is subject to dispute. Where you cannot reach agreement, the areas of disagreement must be clearly identified.

The outcome of an appraisal, a supervision session, a disciplinary hearing or a grievance hearing should be a clear decision or set of decisions – to take specific action, to set a target, to provide training, to issue a warning or to dismiss the allegation, for example. The most important thing to record is this decision or set of decisions.

You may also need to:

- record the background or reason for the decision – for example the behaviour or performance issue that has led to it;
- show that you have been fair, that an individual got a fair hearing and that their views were adequately represented;
- show that you have followed the required steps in the statutory procedure;
- show that all the relevant information was taken into account in reaching the decision.

Your record should be as brief as possible, consistent with the recommendations above. A short, factual record is less likely to provoke disagreement, and is also easier to refer back to in future when progress is being reviewed or a case being appealed.

It is usually a good idea to produce a draft statement which will form the written record once it has been agreed. Ideally the draft would be produced during the meeting, or immediately after it has finished. If this is not practicable, it is vital that the draft be produced as soon as possible, while the events are still fresh in people's minds. Any delay makes it more likely that people will disagree with the record (or want it to say what they now realise they *should* have said, rather than what was actually said).

If the staff member refuses to agree the draft record, you should try to negotiate a mutually acceptable redraft. As a very last resort you should allow them to produce their own version to form part of the record; this is more acceptable than just keeping your version and not allowing them to have their say.

The record should contain:

- a heading to show clearly what the meeting was about and when it happened;
- a list of who was present, and in what capacity;
- a statement setting out each of the issues raised;
- a summary of any evidence put forward and any response given;
- a statement of the decision(s) and any action to be taken.

If, in a disciplinary hearing, for example, the two sides make written submissions, there is no need to repeat these in the record. If the hearing is based on verbal submissions, these must be summed up in writing, in as neutral and dispassionate a way as possible.

You must be especially careful when making records of disciplinary hearings, grievances and appeals, because these are particularly likely to be subject to external scrutiny if the employee is not satisfied with the outcome and takes their case to a tribunal or to court.

Supervision

Supervision is, ideally, a process whereby managers work constructively with individuals and teams to achieve work objectives through joint planning, problem solving, monitoring and evaluation. Supervision sessions are usually carried out between a line manager and an individual in their team, and should normally include an opportunity for employees to give constructive feedback to their manager. They typically cover areas such as:

- whether the individual is up-to-date with their annual leave and TOIL;
- dealing with requests for annual leave or other time off;
- a review of individual performance and objectives;
- feedback to the manager on support provided and ideas or suggestions;
- a discussion of any team issues affecting the individual's performance;
- identification of any health and safety issues or risks;
- identification of the individual's training needs;
- setting objectives (usually mutually agreed) for the individual in future.

When recording objectives it is important that they are specific, clear, and ideally measurable, and that any time-scales are clear and realistic.

General standards that the individual is expected to meet should be distinguished from objectives. They might cover issues such as clarifying the boundaries of the role, understanding the confidentiality policy, confirming responsibilities or setting expectations for the quality or volume of work. They need not be time-bound.

Information that is disclosed by a staff member may sometimes be sensitive or personal. It may be appropriate to discuss whether it is necessary to record this information, and if so what is the best way to do it. However, where the information disclosed impacts on their ability to do the job it will usually be necessary to record the information in some way. It may be appropriate to make a separate, confidential note, but the information *must not* be kept secret by the line manager. The personnel department must not be kept in the dark about any issue affecting an employee, since action may need to be taken, for which complete and accurate records are required.

A copy of the supervision session record should be held by the individual, by their line manager and on the central personnel file.

During a supervision session the manager might start to feel that a problem cannot be resolved. They must resist the temptation to take disciplinary action of any kind on the spot, without going through the formal procedure; this would be disastrous. The supervision record must indicate that the problem was identified but remedial action could not be agreed and leave it at that. The manager would then be free to institute disciplinary proceedings in accordance with your policy (which must, of course, meet the statutory minimum).

Appraisal

Staff appraisal is a process of evaluating an individual's performance in a job against objectives and agreed targets over a period of time, usually 12 months. It obviously has much in common with supervision, but several key differences.

- It looks at things over a longer time-scale, and can include an element of career development.
- It looks ahead as well as backwards.
- It is not so concerned with resolving immediate work difficulties.
- It compares the individual's overall performance with the needs of the job, and may result in changes to the person's duties, either to give them more responsibility if they are doing well or less if they are struggling (or if the job is badly defined).
- It may represent a formal acknowledgement of good performance.
- Appraisal can be linked to pay in the commercial sector, but this is not regarded as normal practice in most voluntary organisations.

A record of the appraisal interview should be structured similarly to that for a supervision session, and could cover:

- highlights, low lights and key achievements of the past year;
- feedback from the manager, on behalf of the organisation;
- a review of training undertaken over the year, and the effect it has had;
- a review of supervision arrangements and any issues the individual has with their team or line manager;
- a review of the job description, to ensure it is still appropriate;
- a discussion on the individual's strengths, areas for development and career aspirations;

- setting overall objectives for the coming year, including training and development needs;
- comments from the employee.

Training records

You must keep records of any training you provide for your staff, for several reasons:

- so that you know whether they have the specific skills and knowledge to do their job;
- to help plan their future training;
- so that you can keep track of what your training budget is being spent on; and
- to help the staff member build up a record of their skills and knowledge.

The most important place to keep a record of training is in each personnel file, because you need to see the whole picture of that person's training. Every time someone goes on a work-related course this should be noted, including any attendance at in-house training or briefing courses, and any courses that they pay for themselves, even if you don't give them time off to attend.

This could be just a simple record of their attendance and any formal qualification obtained, but it might also be useful to keep at least a course outline so that you know a bit more about what they covered.

Training needs are often identified during supervision. 'Training' could include a wide variety of different activities, including:

- short courses on specific topics or skills, in house or external;
- longer courses, generally leading to a qualification;
- self-directed study, computer-based learning and open access courses;
- one-to-one support or coaching or non-managerial supervision, for example with colleagues, mentors or action-learning sets;
- secondment to other teams or other organisations.

All these are worth recording, since they all contribute – or should contribute – to the effectiveness of your staff.

If you have a specific person or team arranging all aspects of staff development, they may want to hold the primary records on training they have been involved in organising. However, each personnel file should still have a summary of that individual's training activities. If necessary you will need to set up a system to ensure that the personnel files are updated whenever someone receives training and that the training department is informed of anything undertaken outside their auspices.

What you must not do is to mix up information about the administration of your training budget and training activities with the information about individual participation in training activities. You will almost certainly need to keep records of your training administration, of course, but this must be separate from the personnel records. If the information about who participated in a course is mixed up with all the details of the room booking, correspondence with the trainer, copies of the handouts and so on, it will not be easily available to any manager who needs to see what training the person has undertaken or to the individual themselves.

It is possible, therefore, to end up with information relating to training in two or even three different places, for different purposes: in the individual personnel files, possibly in separate training department files, and in your training administration files. If your records are held electronically, of course, it should be possible to get the system to hold the information just once and make it available in different formats for these different purposes, but the principle remains: a full record of each individual's training must be easily available as part of their individual records.

Disciplinary procedures

Good practice on disciplinary procedures is available from Acas. Disciplinary proceedings may be taken in two types of circumstance:

- where a problem has persisted, despite efforts to resolve it during supervision or appraisal sessions; or
- where misconduct has taken place which is so serious that it has to be dealt with immediately.

'Gross misconduct' is the most serious kind of offence, and may result in immediate dismissal. Where there is any scope for doubt, it is best to specify in your policies the types of misconduct which will be liable to immediate dismissal. ('Immediate' is not instant: the dismissal must still be legally fair, which means that the individual's side of the story must still be properly heard and the statutory dismissal procedure must be followed.) In cases of gross misconduct your procedure may allow you to suspend the person while the procedure is underway, in which case you must be very careful to communicate with them efficiently. (Note that if you might wish to suspend without pay, this must be a term in the contract of employment.) If they are at home on suspension you must allow time for paperwork to reach them in the post, or you must get their agreement to receive documents at their personal e-mail address.

All disciplinary matters must be documented properly from the outset. Acas recommends that the record of a disciplinary matter should include:

- the complaint against the staff member;
- the staff member's defence;
- findings made and action taken;
- the reason(s) for the action;
- whether an appeal was lodged;
- the outcome of the appeal; and
- subsequent developments.

You should get complaints or evidence in writing if this is possible. If you need to interview witnesses to an incident you should ask them afterwards to write up a brief, signed statement, or you should write a summary of what they have said – using their own words as closely as possible – and ask them to sign it once they agree that it is an accurate representation. If there is a dispute over any documents, such as an allegation of a falsified financial record, for example, you should use the original document, putting a copy in its place if necessary for record-keeping purposes.

Copies of all communications to and from the individual or anyone representing them must be kept, and if contact is made by telephone or verbally it is worth confirming the conversation in writing immediately afterwards. It might be best to print off any e-mails, so that all the material is held in one place.

The file should, of course, be treated as highly confidential, kept under lock and key by the person who is investigating the case and arranging for the disciplinary meeting.

In preparing for a meeting you may want to obtain records of the individual's past performance or behaviour, but this must be proportionate and you must only make use of information from people's files if it is relevant to the issue at hand. You must not allow general dissatisfaction with the person, or issues which have been dealt with already, to cloud your consideration of the immediate case.

Whatever action you take, you must be able to show that the individual was:

- told the nature of the issue;
- told the possible outcome, especially if this could be dismissal;
- reminded of the key features of the process (including, for example, their right to be accompanied by a supporter or union representative at any meetings);
- given a reasonable amount of time to prepare their response;
- given a fair hearing;
- given a fair sanction, if appropriate.

Your record of a disciplinary meeting should follow the guidelines laid down in the 'Recording performance management meetings with individual staff' section above.

If the outcome of the disciplinary case is a warning, the record of the meeting must show this. You should also write a specific letter to the individual warning them that their work or conduct is unsatisfactory. The letter must include:

- the type of conduct or inadequate performance;
- the facts found;
- whether there is a disciplinary penalty in addition to the warning;
- if appropriate, what changes or improvements are expected;
- the time period for the change or improvement, and when and how it will be reviewed;
- the consequences of further misconduct or lack of improvement;
- any right of appeal and the timetable for appeal;
- the date after which the warning will be disregarded if work or performance improves and there is no further disciplinary problem (or the fact that the warning will stay permanently on record).

This applies even if you are giving a 'verbal warning'. A verbal warning does not, in fact, mean just something that is said; it represents the first level of warning. Your letter might say, 'Following the disciplinary hearing, you have received a verbal warning about ...'.

The next two levels of warning are a 'written warning' and a 'final written warning'. For serious misconduct the first warning issued may be a written or final written warning, so it is important that your letter spells out the implications. In particular, a final written warning must include the statement that if no improvement occurs the next step will be dismissal. Final written warnings may be kept on file indefinitely.

The whole file on a disciplinary hearing should be kept by the manager responsible for the hearing until the time for any appeal has elapsed. It should then be passed to the personnel department.

Appeals

The individual might, of course, want to appeal against the outcome of a disciplinary hearing. Your disciplinary procedure must, by law, allow for appeals, and it must comply with at least the statutory minimum. For more information on this, and guidance on who should conduct the appeal, consult the Acas web site.

The grounds of appeal must be one or more of the following:

- that the finding or the penalty were unfair; or
- that there is new evidence which was not available to the original hearing; or

- that there was a flaw in the original process, such as failure to follow procedures or failure to give the person a fair hearing.

The complete file on the case so far should be passed across to the person hearing or chairing the appeal. However, they may need to restrict their consideration of the material, depending on the grounds of appeal. If the claim is that the process was flawed, for example, the appeal should only look at those aspects of the documents in the file that relate to the process.

The record of an appeal hearing should again follow the guidelines laid down in the 'Recording performance management meetings with individual staff' section above, and should be very clear about the outcome, which could be:

- confirmation of the original outcome in full;
- over-ruling the original outcome and rescinding the sanction;
- confirming the decision in principle but reducing the sanction (for example because of mitigating circumstances).

If the sanction is rescinded or amended, you should write to the staff member withdrawing the original letter and setting out the new outcome. (In order to document the procedure, however, you should still keep a copy of the original letter.) If the original finding is upheld, a letter should be sent confirming that this was the outcome of the appeal. When the staff member has reached the end of the appeals procedure, your letter should make this clear. The file should then be transferred to the personnel department.

If the outcome of a disciplinary hearing or appeal is that employment is terminated, this must formally be a decision of the legal employer, normally the board of trustees or management committee. In addition, advice should be taken from the personnel department before writing to the employee. This is to ensure that:

- the dismissal is fair, legally;
- the record reflects properly a fair reason for dismissal; and
- the staff member is told accurately the reason for dismissal, both verbally and in the confirmation letter;
- an authorised person signs the letter of dismissal.

It is important not to make a blanket specification in your disciplinary procedure about how long records will stay on people's files. The decision should be part of the outcome of the disciplinary process, based on the nature of the problem and how long it might be expected to take to resolve it. Typical periods might be:

- verbal warning: six months;
- written warning: 6–12 months;
- final written warning: 12 months or more.

What you must be clear about is: will you actually remove the warning from the file after that time, or just disregard it in future? Whichever you do, you must be clear to the individual what will happen; you do not want them thinking that the warning will be removed, only to find it still on the file when they make a subject access request.

Grievance procedures

You must, by law, have a procedure under which employees can raise any grievance they have about their treatment by their employer or by their colleagues. Minor problems should normally be dealt with informally, after being raised in supervision. By the time the formal grievance procedure is invoked the employee is likely to feel that matters are serious. This must be reflected in how you handle, and how you record, the grievance.

There are many similarities between the principles underlying a grievance procedure and those already discussed in relation to disciplinary procedures.

You should ask the person raising a grievance to put it in writing, if they have not already done so. Encourage them to be as specific as possible about the behaviour or treatment they are complaining about. Where the matter concerns a number of related incidents (each of which on its own may be relatively minor), encourage them to keep a diary, with dates and times, so that the pattern becomes clear.

Collect any additional evidence if necessary, either in documents or through interviews with witnesses which are recorded in signed statements. Keep copies of any correspondence between you and the individual or their representative.

You must have a meeting with the employee (at which they have the right to be accompanied), issue your findings in writing and give them the right of appeal. There is a statutory normal three-stage grievance procedure and a modified statutory two-stage procedure for use in special circumstances. This is where the normal procedure would apply but the employee has left employment and still needs to start or complete an internal grievance before they can make a claim to an employment tribunal. These procedures can be found on the Acas web site.

Your record of a meeting to hear a grievance should follow the guidelines laid down in the 'Recording performance management meetings with individual staff' section above.

Time recording

You do not have to record the comings and goings of your staff, or the time they spend working, but you may need to for one or more of the following reasons.

- If you need to know, for fire safety reasons, who is in the building.
- If you pay staff by the hour.
- If there is a possibility that any of your staff might get near the 48-hour limit in the Working Time Regulations (assuming they have not signed a waiver).
- If people are eligible for overtime payments and you need to calculate what is due.
- If you need to record overtime so that you can give people TOIL.
- If people work irregular hours and would otherwise lose track of how much time they were putting in.
- If you are concerned about absenteeism and people not turning up on time or leaving early.
- If you need to allocate staff hours to specific projects or activities for funding or commercial reasons.

If any of these reasons apply, you must have an appropriate recording system, and it must be fair and consistent. You should either have a time-recording system that applies to everyone, or you should have one that applies to groups of staff for clearly justifiable reasons, to do with the nature of their work.

Ideally you should never single out an individual for time recording when this requirement does not apply to their colleagues. If you do, you must be able to show that the need has been established in supervision, because of specific concerns, and there must be a specific target – for example to reduce lateness to no more than one hour a week over the coming three months.

There are several options for time recording, depending on your main purpose for doing it. You should be clear about what the purpose is, then choose the method that is most appropriate. For example, you may use one or more of the following.

- A simple in/out board, or a daily tick-sheet for staff to show that they have arrived, and then that they have left.
- A swipe card system to combine building security with records of staff attendance (provided, of course, that staff realise that the data is used for this purpose).
- Individual time sheets which staff have to fill in, showing when they started work each day and when they finished, broken down, if it is relevant, by project or client.
- An overtime log which staff only fill in when they work outside their specified hours.

- A reporting system so that staff who arrive after a specified time have their lateness noted by their line manager on their absence card (see Appendix J).
- A traditional clocking-in system.

Whatever system you use, it is only worth doing (and only fair on all staff) if you insist that people record their time accurately. It should be made clear that they are expected to do this, and any consistent failure to comply should be followed up in supervision.

Time records should only be kept as long as there is a need. For example, if you review time sheets at each supervision session and the individual and their line manager agree on the figures, the totals (of overtime earned or TOIL taken, for example) can be recorded in the supervision record and all the time sheets destroyed. If the issue is merely to be aware of who is in the building in case of fire, you could use a new sheet every day.

Monitoring staff: general concerns

The Information Commissioner's Code of Practice Part 3 is concerned with all aspects of monitoring staff by the employer. Unlike Parts 1 and 2 it does not have a set of benchmarks supported by a discussion. Instead, there is the full Code, a supplement looking at specific questions in more detail, and a summary for small and medium enterprises.

> ### Information Commissioner's core principles on monitoring
> - It will usually be intrusive to monitor your workers.
> - Workers have legitimate expectations that they can keep their personal lives private and that they are also entitled to a degree of privacy in the work environment.
> - If employers wish to monitor their workers, they should be clear about the purpose and satisfied that the particular monitoring arrangement is justified by real benefits that will be delivered.
> - Workers should be aware of the nature, extent and reasons for any monitoring, unless (exceptionally) covert monitoring is justified.
> - In any event, workers' awareness will influence their expectations.

In most voluntary organisations very little monitoring is likely to take place. In its section on good practice the Code covers the following.

1 Managing data protection.
2 The general approach to monitoring.
3 Monitoring electronic communications.
4 Video and audio monitoring.

5   Covert monitoring.

6   In-vehicle monitoring.

7   Monitoring through information from third parties.

Among the Commissioner's general considerations are the following points, in brief.

■ Monitoring must be properly authorised.

■ The impact on people's privacy must be fully justified by the benefits.

■ If monitoring is to be used to enforce your rules and standards, these must be set out clearly; staff must be aware of what they are and that they will be monitored.

■ You must tell staff what monitoring is taking place and why.

■ Information obtained through monitoring must be kept to a minimum and held under strict security.

■ Information collected through monitoring must not be used for anything else, unless 'it is clearly in the worker's interest to do so or it reveals activity that no reasonable employer could be expected to ignore'.

Here we give a brief outline of points to consider in specific cases and then discuss equal opportunities monitoring and monitoring of electronic communications in more detail, since these are the areas likely to be of most interest to the majority of voluntary organisations. We would refer readers to the full Code (or the small business summary) for further information on this and all other aspects of monitoring.

Video monitoring of staff, in order to maintain standards, should normally be kept separate from Closed Circuit TV (CCTV) systems whose main purpose is security. If visitors or customers may inadvertently be captured by monitoring they must be informed. CCTV systems are subject to a separate Code of Practice (available on the Information Commissioner's web site, see the Resources section on page 186), which is outside the scope of this book.

Covert monitoring (without people's knowledge) should only happen where it is really the only option, and only where you suspect criminal activity. The aim should be to collect evidence as quickly as possible and then hand the whole matter over to the police. Covert monitoring must not be used where it would be especially intrusive such as in toilets or offices allocated for private use.

Monitoring information about employees' or workers' private lives (such as carrying out credit checks) should usually be avoided.

Equal opportunities monitoring

Many organisations monitor the make-up of their staff and/or their job applicants, and this is often expected by outside bodies such as funders.

It takes you time and effort to collect the information for monitoring, then it takes time and effort to analyse it. It takes time and effort for people to provide the information and they may find it intrusive. On all counts, therefore, you should make sure that you carry out monitoring only when you really need to do so, that you collect only the information you really need, and that you treat the information you do collect carefully.

Discrimination can take two broad forms, which may or may not exist together: your organisation might treat a whole group of people disadvantageously on the basis of their sex, race or disability, for example; or you may treat a particular individual unfairly. The purpose of monitoring is to investigate the first of these.

The best monitoring is designed to identify any underlying need for change. It may reveal a pattern which is not so obvious when you consider individuals on their own; this could – indeed should – lead to changes which will address any discrimination which is found. You might then monitor the same issue over a period of time to show how things are changing in response to the changes in your policies or procedures.

What is important is your organisation's actual behaviour. You may already know that your staff are unrepresentative of the area you work in, or of your client group, or that certain types of people don't end up as managers. If it is that obvious, you don't need to carry out monitoring; you need to take action. Monitoring is only worth carrying out where the organisation may be unaware of areas where it is acting unfairly, or where you need hard statistics, either for a base-line picture of the situation or to track changes over time.

In all cases you have to choose between collecting information once, retaining it, and reusing it for each instance of monitoring, or collecting it anew each time. The main advantage of the first option is that you do not have to keep going back to your staff for more information. However, you run the risk that you will be keeping information longer than you need it – especially if your future requirements are vague. You also have to consider whether the information (or your staff team) might have changed in the meantime; if so, in order to be accurate you would have to ask again anyway.

Because of this, your starting point for equal opportunities monitoring must be to have a clear idea of what you are trying to achieve. If you can achieve the same ends in a way that is less intrusive than monitoring, that is the better course of action. If you are sure that you do need to carry out monitoring, decide whether it is a one-off exercise (or sufficiently infrequent to be treated as a one-off), or part of your routine.

You must not use information for monitoring purposes unless the individual knows that you are going to do so. In particular, do not use information for monitoring which you have also collected for other purposes, without saying so. For example you may know (or assume that you know) the sex of each of your staff members, so that you do not need to ask; that is not enough, you must make them aware of your intentions.

Because monitoring usually involves highly personal information you should always collect it directly from the individual. It is very poor practice to guess (especially if they have refused to provide information) or to extrapolate from other information you have, such as their name. Even if you are confident that a name reveals someone's racial or ethnic origin, for example, you must allow them to choose how to categorise themselves, if they are willing to be categorised.

Where you have decided to collect information to use in regular monitoring exercises, you may as well collect it, and explain the purpose, at the time people join your organisation. You may then keep it on file, but you should be very careful to keep it confidential. You should give people the chance to update their information, or check that it is accurate, from time to time. (For example, even if you have subsequently learned of a disability, you must allow the person to decide for themselves whether to be classified as disabled for monitoring purposes.)

If people do not want you to use information about them for monitoring purposes you should – and in most cases must – respect their wishes. If you already have the information, when you alert people to the monitoring you must give them the opportunity to say that they do not want you to use the data you hold for monitoring purposes. When you are collecting it they must have the option not to provide information for monitoring purposes.

When you publish or pass on your statistics you should consider whether you are at risk of inadvertently disclosing information about individuals unnecessarily. Where figures are very low – perhaps just one member of staff falls into a particular category – it may be better to give the information as 'under 10 per cent' or 'fewer than 5 per cent' rather than the actual number.

In summary, therefore, you must:

- collect monitoring information only where there is a clear, justifiable need;
- collect only the kinds of information you really need;
- tell people you are collecting, or using, their data for monitoring purposes;
- collect the information directly from individuals and allow them to define themselves;
- allow people to update their information as often as necessary;
- respect anyone's wish not to have their data used for monitoring;
- store monitoring information carefully so that it remains confidential;
- be careful how you release statistics.

The detailed background to the discussion above reveals that there are subtle differences between different kinds of equal opportunities monitoring information. In practice these can be largely ignored, provided you follow the highest standards in respect of all monitoring, but you may find it useful in some cases to know your options more precisely.

The table below shows the main areas in which voluntary organisations typically may want to carry out equal opportunities monitoring. Most are related to anti-discrimination legislation, and many are 'sensitive' in terms of Data Protection (see Chapter 3). Both of these factors may affect how you approach your monitoring.

	Discrimination prohibited by law?	'Sensitive'	Special Data Protection provisions?
Sex	Yes	No	Not applicable
Ethnic or racial origin	Yes	Yes	Yes
Disability	Yes	Yes	Yes
Religion	Yes	Yes	Yes
Criminal record	Yes	Yes	No
Sexual orientation	Yes	Yes	No
Trade union membership	Yes	Yes	No
Marital status	Yes	No	Not applicable
Age	Not until 2006	No	Not applicable
Where people live*	No	No	Not applicable
* In order to show, for example, that you are not recruiting from a restricted area.			

The requirement for individuals to know that you are using data about them for monitoring applies in all cases. In addition you have to meet one of the 'Schedule 2' Conditions and, for 'sensitive' data, also one of the 'Schedule 3' Conditions. In all cases, you meet the Conditions if you have consent from the individual. The simplest course of action is therefore to get consent.

Consent for using 'sensitive' data has to be 'explicit'. It is not entirely clear whether this means it has to be in writing, but this may be advisable. If you are following the recommendation above always to collect information directly from the individual, it is not hard to get consent. Your forms, after explaining why you are carrying out the monitoring and encouraging people to complete the form, could say something like: 'You do not have to give us this information, and will not be penalised if you withhold it. If you do provide information we will take this as consent for us to use it for monitoring purposes.'

In addition to saying that the information does not have to be provided, you could reinforce this by providing a 'Do not wish to say' box within each category. If you do this, and people go ahead and give you the information, it is generally safe to assume that you have their consent. (Note that consent can be withdrawn. If people subsequently change their mind you cannot continue to use the information.)

You do not necessarily need consent for non-'sensitive' data or for 'sensitive' data where there is special provision. However, you do have to provide safeguards for the individual which, in effect, give them the right to opt out.

You could use non-'sensitive' data for monitoring without consent, provided you meet the sixth fair processing Condition: that the use is in your 'legitimate interests' and you are not harming the data subject. In order to be sure that you are causing no harm, you should be satisfied that the individual knows what you are doing and has been given the opportunity to opt out if it is likely to cause them a problem.

In the cases of ethnic or racial origin, disability or religion, there are special provisions stating that you do not need consent. These are set out in Paragraph 9 of Schedule 3 in the Act, in the case of racial or ethnic origin; Paragraph 7 of Statutory Instrument 2000 No. 417 in the case of disability or religion. However, the data must be used for genuine monitoring purposes only (not for making decisions about the individual, for example), and if they tell you in writing to stop using it you must do so. (Technically this only applies in the case of disability or religion, but for ethnic and racial origin you must have 'appropriate safeguards for the rights and freedoms of Data Subjects' which suggests that it would certainly be good practice to stop if asked to do so.)

For the 'sensitive' data where there is no special provision, it is hard to see how you could meet any of the 'Schedule 3' Conditions other than 'explicit' consent from the data subject.

The result of this is that, when you collect information for monitoring purposes you are likely to have sufficient consent for any data the individual provides as long as you have given the kind of information and reassurance suggested above. For 'sensitive' data you have to be aware that people have the absolute right to refuse consent, or to withdraw consent subsequently, or to tell you not to use the data – which amounts to the same thing. You cannot force people to provide monitoring data about themselves, or allow you to use data you already hold, however keen your funders or other agencies might be for you to collect it and provide statistics.

Monitoring electronic communications

Monitoring telephone calls and e-mails is subject to the Lawful Business Practice Regulations, under the Regulation of Investigatory Powers Act 2000. Among the purposes for which monitoring is allowed are:

> *'Monitoring or keeping a record of communications in order to ascertain compliance with regulatory or self-regulatory practices or procedures [which apply to the system controller's business].'*

This provision would be used to demonstrate that you are complying with legal requirements or official codes of practice, for example if you must give people specific information as part of your transaction, or if you must obtain consent for a particular course of action. The code of practice you are following must be 'published by ... a body ... which includes amongst its objectives the publication of standards or codes of practice for the conduct of business'.

> *'Monitoring or keeping a record of communications in order to ascertain or demonstrate the standards [expected] of persons using the system in the course of their duties.'*

This is the 'quality control' provision. It could be used where you are following an internal code of practice that doesn't have the official status which would count for the case above, and where you want to monitor the quality of someone's work. It would also cover training. Circumstances where it would probably be acceptable not to have the caller's consent would include:

- a supervisor listening in to check that someone is answering calls to the organisation's standards;
- recording calls so that you can play them back to help a telephone operator see where they could improve;
- arranging for new recruits to listen in to an experienced call handler.

However, you must be careful not to be intrusive, and you should normally consider seeking the caller's consent where:

- the call is to be recorded and used for wider training purposes; or
- you allow other people (such as trustees) to listen in.

Best practice is only to use genuinely anonymous recordings, or better still acted out scenarios rather than live calls, for training purposes.

> *'Monitoring or keeping a record of communications for the purpose of preventing or detecting crime.'*

There is nothing in the Regulations that restricts this to the police. If you suspect that a member of staff may be defrauding you or otherwise committing a crime you may be able to intercept their phone calls, but only where the action is proportionate and justified in all the circumstances.

'Monitoring or keeping a record of communications for the purpose of investigating or detecting the unauthorised use of [any] telecommunication system.'

This apparently gives you very wide powers. As with the crime purpose, however, your actions must be proportionate. While it might be reasonable, for example, to record the numbers dialled by each member of staff (if your system enables this), it would not be acceptable to listen to calls in without very good reason.

Remember that you can't easily discipline someone for doing something that wasn't self-evidently wrong unless you have told them that you consider it wrong. You may have to prove that they knew it was wrong. Also 'unauthorised' implies that you have to say what is and isn't authorised; the Regulations don't say 'unacceptable', for example. You would therefore be wise to set out in your staff handbook the behaviour you expect, and ensure that everyone has seen and understood it.

Information Commissioner's general recommendations on monitoring electronic communications

1 Establish a policy on the use of electronic communications and communicate it to workers.
2 Ensure that where monitoring involves the interception of a communication it is not outlawed by the Regulation of Investigatory Powers Act 2000.
3 Make an impact assessment to determine what, if any, monitoring of electronic communications is justified by the benefits. Limit the scope of monitoring to what is strictly required to deliver those benefits.

Listening in to phone calls is, by any standards, intrusive. If you can fully justify the need, the main thing is to ensure that everyone involved (your staff and the people they are talking to) know that monitoring is happening, or possible. Take advice, for example from the Telephone Helplines Association, if you are in any doubt (see the Resources section on page 186).

Information Commissioner's recommendations on telephone monitoring

4   Ensure that the assessment of whether monitoring is justified takes account of the specific circumstances of telephone monitoring.

5   Ensure that those making calls to or receiving calls from workers, as well as workers themselves, are aware of any monitoring and the purpose behind it, unless this is obvious.

6   Ensure that workers are aware of the extent to which you receive information about the use of telephone lines in their homes, or mobile phones provided for their personal use, for which your business pays partly or fully. Do not make use of information about personal calls for monitoring.

Opening e-mails when staff are away has been discussed in the previous chapter. You may also want to check up on what people are saying in e-mails, on whether they are using your e-mail and other internet facilities inappropriately, or on whether they are accessing inappropriate web sites. All of these are possible, if there is a good reason, but must be done with very careful regard to privacy.

This means, for example, that it is better to use automated systems to block access to inappropriate web sites or to filter out unacceptable e-mails. It means warning users that their e-mail and internet use is not necessarily completely private, while reassuring them that intrusion will be kept to a minimum. And, where limited private use of your facilities is allowed, it means giving them a means of distinguishing private e-mails from work ones. A sample AUP can be found in Appendix N.

Information Commissioner's recommendations on e-mail and internet access monitoring

7   Ensure that the assessment of whether monitoring is justified takes account of the specific circumstances of e-mail and/or internet access monitoring.

8   Make those sending e-mails to workers, as well as workers themselves, aware of any monitoring and the purpose behind it, unless this is obvious.

9   If it is necessary to check the e-mail accounts of workers in their absence, make sure that they are aware that this will happen.

10 Inform workers of the extent to which information about their internet access and e-mails is retained in the system and for how long.

11 In reviewing the results of any monitoring take into account the possibility of unintentional access of web sites by workers.

Chapter summary

If, following good practice, you have a system of supervision and appraisal, this must be documented properly. Outcomes must be recorded clearly, and the employee should be asked to indicate their agreement with the accuracy of the record.

A record of training undertaken and qualifications gained should be kept in each employee's file, in addition to any central training administration files.

Disciplinary procedures, grievance procedures and appeals must be carefully recorded, in order to show that they have been properly and fairly conducted. The record of the outcome must be complete, without being over-long, and all the records must be able to withstand external scrutiny if necessary.

If you need to record attendance for all or some of your staff, the requirement must be imposed fairly and you should think about what method of time recording best meets your needs.

Monitoring of staff and their activities should be carried out only in accordance with the Information Commissioner's Code of Practice on monitoring. Monitoring of e-mails and phone calls must also comply with the Lawful Business Practice Regulations.

Equal opportunities monitoring must take account of the fact that the data is likely to be 'sensitive'. It must be done for a clear purpose, with the knowledge of the individuals concerned, and with the option for them not to answer any question if they choose not to.

For table, see over.

Document	Main requirements	Retention period	File location
Supervision notes	Agreed by line manager and employee	Until next appraisal	Personnel file, with copy held by employee and line manager
Appraisal record	Agreed by manager conducting interview and employee	6 months after employment ends	Personnel file, with copy held by employee and line manager
Individual training record	Complete and up-to-date	Until employment ends, and then if required as backing for references	Personnel file (in addition to that held for training administration)
Disciplinary, grievance or appeal case file	Accuracy and fairness	Until no possibility exists of appeal, tribunal, court case or child protection/POVA investigation	Personnel department
Disciplinary or appeal case outcome and any letter containing a warning	Clarity and completeness, so that the issue can be fully understood in future	6 years after employment ends	Personnel file (confidential)
Grievance case outcome	Brief summary	Until no possibility of appeal (or external case) exists	Personnel file (confidential)
Time recording	Appropriate to the business need	Until agreed at end of suitable period	Personnel file
Equal opportunities monitoring data	With knowledge and consent of individual	While employed (should be periodically checked with employee)	Personnel file or central records

chapter 13

DISCLOSING INFORMATION ABOUT PERSONNEL

An organisation frequently has to disclose information about its staff. Many of these disclosures will be obvious and non-controversial. However, you should be aware that any disclosure at all could be potentially harmful, depending on the circumstances. Where a couple have split up, for example, it might be wholly inappropriate to reveal to the ex-partner your staff member's current address, or even whether they are present in the office at any given time. Disclosing a telephone number, revealing someone's movements, or even publishing a photograph in which they appear may be less innocuous than you realise.

For this reason you need to be clear with your staff about the circumstances in which you will disclose information concerning them and any precautions you will take. You need to give them clear and straightforward opportunities to alert you to any additional restrictions they feel are necessary in order to protect their interests or prevent harm.

Then, of course, you have to ensure that all staff who handle information about their colleagues comply with these precautions. The need for a security culture and for clarity on confidentiality have been discussed in Chapter 4, but it is worth reiterating here that you have a responsibility for making staff sensitive at all times to the various ways in which private information about their colleagues might leak out into inappropriate hands. The most important considerations are these.

- Do you have personnel procedures that are designed to involve the least necessary disclosure of private information?
- Do you actively warn staff not to disclose private information about colleagues casually over the telephone or in gossip, and to be aware of deliberate attempts to trick them into giving information away?
- Do you have a robust procedure for authorising disclosures when it is necessary, so that staff are never left guessing or responding in panic?

Information Commissioner's benchmarks on disclosure requests

1 Establish a disclosure policy to tell staff who are likely to receive requests for information about workers how to respond, and to where they should refer requests that fall outside the policy rules.

2 Ensure that disclosure decisions that are not covered by clear policy rules are only taken by staff who are familiar with the Act and this Code, and who are able to give the decision proper consideration.

3 Unless you are under a legal obligation to do so, only disclose information about a worker where you conclude that in all the circumstances it is fair to do so. Bear in mind that the duty of fairness is owed primarily to the worker. Where possible take account of the worker's views. Only disclose confidential information if the worker has clearly agreed.

4 Where a disclosure is requested in an emergency, make a careful decision as to whether to disclose, taking into account the nature of the information being requested and the likely impact on the worker of not providing it.

5 Make staff aware that those seeking information sometimes use deception to gain access to it. Ensure that they check the legitimacy of any request and the identity and authority of the person making it.

6 Ensure that if you intend to disclose sensitive personal data, a sensitive data condition is satisfied.

7 Where the disclosure would involve a transfer of information about a worker to a country outside the European Economic Area, ensure that there is a proper basis for making the transfer.

8 Inform the worker before or as soon as is practicable after a request has been received that a non-regular disclosure is to be made, unless prevented by law from doing so, or unless this would constitute a 'tip off' prejudicing a criminal or tax investigation.

9 Keep a record of non-regular disclosures. Regularly check and review this record to ensure that the requirements of the Act are being satisfied.

Routine disclosures

The main considerations in deciding whether any disclosure is appropriate are:

■ are the staff sufficiently aware it is happening? and

■ do they have any choice in the matter – in other words do we have to allow them to opt out, or do we need their active permission?

Where a disclosure is completely obvious and routine you are unlikely to have to inform your staff or give them a choice. This would apply, for instance, to information which you must by law provide to the Inland Revenue. It would also apply to staff being identified to professional colleagues in other organisations: if a member of your staff attends a meeting on your organisation's behalf it would almost always be rude and unhelpful for them not to provide their name and work contact details, and it would be reasonable for you to insist that they cannot remain anonymous. You would have to have a very serious security concern (or very serious mistrust of the other participants' commitment to confidentiality) to consider working anonymously.

You may decide that you do need to inform staff in less obvious cases, but without giving them a choice because you believe that the disclosure is essential. This might apply, for example, where you need to give details of the qualifications and salaries of the staff who would deliver a service, as part of a funding application. Unless you tell your staff that you are doing this, they will not be aware of the disclosure.

Identifying staff to the public

Where staff are dealing directly with the public, in particular, there may be cases where they have a good reason for being unwilling to identify themselves. You should give proper consideration to any concerns that they have; you do not want to endanger your staff through insisting on identifying them when this is inappropriate, either in relation to that particular person's circumstances or because the nature of the work suggests that they might attract hostility.

This does not mean, however, that staff have a veto. If there are sound reasons for wanting staff to identify themselves and you are satisfied that the risk to them is minimal, you may decide to insist. However, a compromise that can be used is to allow staff to use a pseudonym if they wish. This enables them to retain a friendly approach, and enables the public to identify who they have been talking to for future reference, while protecting the staff member's actual identity.

> **Information Commissioner's benchmarks on publication and other disclosures**
> 1   Only publish information about workers where:
>   – the information is clearly not intrusive, or
>   – the worker has consented to disclosure, or
>   – the information is in a form that does not identify individual workers.

> 2 Where information about workers is published on the basis of consent, ensure that when the worker gives consent he or she is made aware of the extent of information that will be published, how it will be published and the implications of this.
>
> 3 Only supply personal information about workers to a trade union for its recruitment purposes if:
> – the trade union is recognised by the employer,
> – the information is limited to that necessary to enable a recruitment approach, and
> – each worker has been previously told that this will happen and has been given a clear opportunity to object.
>
> 4 Where staffing information is supplied to trade unions in the course of collective bargaining, ensure the information is such that individual workers cannot be identified.

Photographs of staff

The use of photographs is a particular form of disclosure which frequently causes concern. Some uses are obviously unavoidable, and staff have no choice: your security system, for example, might involve staff wearing badges displaying their photograph. Since they are actually wearing the badges there is no possibility of them being unaware of the disclosure.

In such a case it would almost certainly be reasonable to keep a copy of the photograph in each personnel file, or on computer. However, you would have to be careful not to use the copy subsequently for a purpose that the individual was unaware of. In most cases it would be better to seek consent for the secondary use.

Where photographs are to be published more widely, in a newsletter for example, you should normally tell people beforehand and get their consent, unless there is an over-riding reason not to do this. You should also take account of the fact that people may not object in principle to photographs of them being published but may not be happy with a particular photograph. Regardless of the legalities (because a photograph may not be 'personal data' in terms of the Data Protection Act 1998 – see Chapter 3) it is just not worth jeopardising your staff relationships by upsetting them in this way. Wherever possible you should respect people's preferences in such cases – which is another reason for telling them what you intend to do while there is still time for them to have their say.

A similar argument would apply to the posting of photographs of staff (or for that matter clients or service users) on notice boards. While many people will have no objection, it is better to avoid problems altogether by clearing your actions in advance than offend people and then have to put matters right.

It should go without saying that you should never keep, display or publish photographs of staff that are potentially embarrassing or compromising, whatever the circumstances in which the photograph was taken. Neither should you permit your staff to display or publish such photographs of colleagues, even where they will only be seen by a limited number of people. As the employer you could be liable for harassment, for example, if a member of staff pinned up an inappropriate picture of a colleague, taken at an office party, whether on a notice board or above their own desk.

Identifying staff on your web site

As discussed in the context of Data Protection Principle 8 in Chapter 3 it is important to recognise that web sites are, in effect, more public than other forms of publication, because of their world wide accessibility.

You may well feel that making some details of your staff available to the public on your web site can be more efficient as well as helping to avoid the organisation appearing as a faceless bureaucracy. Good practice would be to inform staff before doing so, and then to be prepared to take seriously any objections they may have.

If it is essential that people be given some means of contacting a specific member of staff who is not happy about being identified, you should consider whether generic contact details can be provided – 'trainingofficer@yourorganisation. org.uk', for example, rather than 'janesmith@yourorganisation.org.uk'.

This approach may be worth considering in any case. It not only avoids any potential problems but also imposes less of a burden in keeping the web site up to date

References (including financial references)

Incoming references during the recruitment process have been discussed in Chapter 8. Outgoing references are frequently a source of uncertainty.

Briefly, the situation is that in most cases there is no legal obligation to provide an employment reference. The main exceptions are in fields where a reference from the most recent previous employer is normal practice, and it would be difficult for anyone to get a job without one. Care services are the most obvious example in the voluntary sector, although the relevant case law related to the financial services industry. If you are obliged – under Care Standards, for example – to seek a reference from the most recent previous employer when you take someone on, then you may well have an implied contractual duty to provide references for any of your staff when they leave.

If you do provide a reference, you owe a duty of care both to the subject of the reference and to the prospective employer. In other words the reference must not be too good, encouraging the employment of an unsuitable candidate, nor inaccurately poor, denying someone the chance to get a job they are suitable for. If you want to give a reference that mentions poor performance you must base this on evidence and the employee must have already been told that their performance is an issue.

You should therefore have a policy on what type of reference you are prepared to provide, and apply this consistently. This could range from none at all (although this is very unusual), through a mere statement of the fact that the person worked for you between certain dates in a certain capacity, up to a full reference with comments on their absence record, quality of work and so on.

Before giving a reference you should satisfy yourself that the individual has given their consent to your disclosure. Normally this will be implicit in the fact that they have provided your details as a referee. However, where you are being asked to include 'sensitive' data – on health or sickness absence, for example – you should check that the individual has given specific consent for this disclosure.

You must ensure that the records you keep when someone leaves are 'adequate, relevant and not excessive' for the purpose of providing whatever level of detail your policy specifies in a reference. This could mean keeping quite detailed records for some time, or it could mean disposing of a lot of raw material and consolidating it onto a single summary sheet (see also Chapter 15.)

Any reference you give must be accurate. In order to demonstrate that the information you provide is accurate, you should be able to substantiate it by referring back to information in your files. It is usually better to give facts and allow the recipient to draw conclusions than to give value judgements. You might, for example, say 'This person had eight days of sickness absence last year' rather than 'This person had a good attendance record'. If you cannot answer specific questions from the information available in your records, say so; don't rely on your own memory or impression unless you are being specifically asked to do so and feel comfortable that you are giving an answer you could justify.

While one would hope that a reference based on good-quality personnel records would meet the test of accuracy, some organisations have a policy of showing draft references to the data subject. As well as enabling you to be confident about the accuracy of what you have put, this should also avoid any subsequent suspicion the data subject may have about whether the content of the reference affected their job chances. If you do have this policy, of course, it must be applied consistently. You must not share 'good' references with the individual but hold back 'bad' ones.

If you give a *confidential* reference (either because it is your policy or because you are specifically asked for one), the data subject does not have the right to see it by means of a subject access request to you. This is a specific provision in the Data Protection Act. They may, however, make a subject access application to the recipient. This data controller then, of course, has to apply the 'third party' rule (see Chapter 5). If your identity would be clear to the data subject, access should not normally be granted without your consent. In order to avoid uncertainty, and to spare the recipient from seeking your consent in the event of a subject access request (which could come many years later), it is good practice to specify when providing a reference whether it is confidential or may be shown to the data subject.

As well as being asked for job references, you may also from time to time be asked to confirm an employee's income or other details, for example in connection with a mortgage application. The key point here is to be certain that the employee wants you to do this. If you are sure that you are doing it at their request, or with their consent, and that they are aware of the type of information being provided, there is nothing to stop you providing the information. You must, of course, ensure that the information you provide is accurate.

You should never give a reference of any sort over the telephone, partly because of the difficulty of knowing for certain whom you are talking to and partly because of the scope for error and the lack of any evidence after the event of what information you have provided. You should never be tempted to give a verbal reference in order to avoid committing uncomplimentary remarks to paper, and no reputable organisation should ask for or accept a verbal reference. If a response by fax or e-mail is asked for, in order to save time, you should only use either of these methods if you have satisfied yourself (if necessary by writing to or phoning the organisation) that the fax number or e-mail address is secure and will not risk a breach of confidentiality.

When giving a reference you should also consider whether you need to verify the identity of the person or organisation who is making the request. You may want to insist that the request is put on headed paper, with the reply to be sent to an address which you can verify independently, perhaps on the organisation's web site. It may also be legitimate to ask for the name of a specific person if the reference request doesn't specify this. Above all, check with your employee (or ex-employee) that they are expecting you to receive a reference request from this source if you have the slightest concern.

Information Commissioner's benchmarks on references

References given:

1 Set out a clear company policy stating who can give corporate references, in what circumstances, and the policy that applies to the granting of access to them. Make anyone who is likely to become a referee aware of this policy.

2 Do not provide confidential references about a worker unless you are sure that this is the worker's wish.

3 Establish at the time a worker's employment ends, whether or not the worker wishes references to be provided to future employers or to others.

References received:

4 When responding to a request from a worker to see his or her own reference, and the reference enables a third party to be identified, make a judgement as to what information it is reasonable to withhold, using the guidelines given [elsewhere] in this Code.

Trade unions, pensions and insurance schemes

Many organisations introduce their staff to trade unions or other organisations which can provide them with benefits, such as pensions or health insurance, and you may also deduct money from salaries on behalf of such external organisations.

Since October 2001 all employers with five or more employees have had to offer some kind of pension, either an occupational pension, a group personal pension or a basic 'stakeholder pension'. For more information consult the Pensions Advisory Service (OPAS) web site (see the Resources section on page 189). You must provide all employees with full details of the pension scheme within two months of their joining, and with other details on request.

When it comes to information about your individual staff, you must make sure that you only disclose information to these external organisations with the knowledge and, normally, the consent of your employees. You must also be very careful to distinguish between information that is relevant to your own relationship with your staff and information about them that you handle on behalf of other organisations. Do not use the latter for any of your own purposes without your employees' knowledge.

In most cases the best solution is to leave everything up to the individual. You provide them with information about the Union or the pension scheme, for example, and leave it up to them to make the contact. If they decide to join, all you then need is enough information to make the appropriate salary deductions and/or employer's contribution.

If for any reason you feel that it would be better to pass details of new employees to the external organisation so that they can make the approach directly, you should take care to inform new employees that this will happen. If they object, you are likely to find difficulty in complying with the 'fair processing conditions', (see Chapter 3) and should therefore not pass their details on.

Information Commissioner's benchmarks on pension and insurance schemes

1   Do not access personal data required by a third party to administer a scheme, in order to use it for general employment purposes.

2   Limit your exchange of information with a scheme provider to the minimum necessary for operation of the scheme bearing in mind the scheme's funding obligations. Make sure that if sensitive data are involved a sensitive data condition is satisfied.

Pension schemes

3   Do not use information gained from the internal trustees or administrators of pension schemes for general employment purposes.

Insurance schemes

4   If your business takes on the role of broker or your staff act as group secretary for a private medical insurance scheme, ensure that personal data gathered are kept to a minimum, limit access to the information and do not use it for general employment purposes.

5   Ensure that when a worker joins a health or insurance scheme it is made clear what, if any, information is to be passed between the scheme controller and the employer and how it will be used.

Marketing

Some employers allow data about their personnel to be used for marketing. This could be for an external company – for example by including information in pay packets – or it could be for your own organisation or a linked trading company – inviting staff to buy their Christmas cards from you or to participate in one of your sponsored events, perhaps.

Regardless of the circumstances, people have an absolute right to opt out of receiving marketing material in any form – on paper, by e-mail or by phone – if it is sent specifically to them. (This does not, however, cover an advertisement placed on a notice board, on your web site, or printed in a newsletter, for example.) Furthermore, in order to be 'fair' in terms of the first Data Protection Principle (see Chapter 3), the Information Commissioner suggests (in the benchmarks quoted below) that staff must give positive consent to their details being passed on to other organisations for marketing purposes, or to their details being subsequently used for types of marketing they were not originally made aware of.

This means that you must at the very least tell personnel if you will be using their details for marketing and give them an easily-exercised opportunity to opt out. Even if someone doesn't opt out initially, they have the right to change their mind and tell you to stop marketing to them, or stop passing their details to other organisations, at any point. Your personnel systems must record their preferences and ensure that these are fully respected.

> **Information Commissioner's benchmarks on marketing**
> 1 Inform new workers if your organisation intends to use their personal information to deliver advertising or marketing messages to them. Give workers a clear opportunity to object (an 'opt-out') and respect any objections whenever received.
> 2 Do not disclose workers' details to other organisations for their marketing unless individual workers have positively and freely indicated their agreement (an 'opt-in').
> 3 If you intend to use details of existing workers for marketing for the first time either in ways that were not explained when they first joined or that they would not expect, do not proceed until individual workers have positively and freely indicated their agreement (an 'opt-in').

Disclosures to the police, lawyers and official bodies

A number of possible situations may arise where you are asked to provide information about a member of your staff, or where you feel the need to inform the authorities.

- An official body may ask for information which you must, by law, provide – such as where the Child Support Agency needs information about an absent parent and cannot get it directly from them.
- You may be required by law to volunteer information – such as in connection with accidents (see RIDDOR, page 115), or when someone for whom you are paying a deduction to the Child Support Agency leaves your employment.
- The police may ask you to help them by providing information, even though you are not obliged to – such as when they suspect that your CCTV system may have captured an incident they are investigating.
- You may have to go to the police or another body such as the Department of Health – for example when you suspect an employee of fraud or some other crime, or have a concern over child protection or the wellbeing of vulnerable adults.

Under the Data Protection Act there is an exemption which allows you to do any of these, even if your action would not normally be compliant – perhaps because the data subject doesn't know you are doing it, or because you are using data for a different purpose from the one you originally specified.

In all cases, however, there are criteria that must be met; otherwise there could be a breach of Data Protection. Where you are under a legal obligation, the disclosure must be 'required' by law, not just permitted. It would be reasonable to expect any agency asking you for information to spell out the legal basis for their request before you comply, in order to satisfy yourself that the law genuinely does require you to provide the information. If they cannot satisfy you that the disclosure is required by law, you can still respond, of course, but only if your disclosure complies with all the Data Protection Principles. In most cases you would therefore need to at least inform the individual concerned and give them the opportunity to tell you if there is any over-riding reason why the disclosure should not be made.

Where you choose to help the police, you are allowed not to comply with most of the Data Protection Principles, provided you are satisfied that failing to disclose would 'prejudice ... the prevention or detection of crime, the apprehension or prosecution of offenders, or the assessment or collection of any tax or duty ...'. You must still meet one of the Schedule 2 Conditions and if applicable one of the Schedule 3 Conditions, however. So, for example, if you rely on the sixth Schedule 2 Condition (see Chapter 3), you must be sure that your legitimate interests (or those of the organisation you disclose to) are sufficient to over-ride the rights, freedoms and legitimate interests of the data subject.

Where the police approach you it would be reasonable to expect their request to be in writing, to state that failure to disclose would prejudice their investigation, and to be reasonably specific about the individual or the situation in which they were interested. 'Fishing trips' may well not comply with the Data Protection Act exemption.

It is normally good practice to inform the individual that a disclosure is being made, unless there is a good reason not to. Because of the danger of tipping someone off when they are being investigated, however, you should consult the police (or social services, or whomever) about whether or not to tell the individual.

You are also allowed to ignore most of the Data Protection Principles if you disclose information to your lawyers in the course of seeking legal advice or taking legal action. There is, therefore, effectively no restriction on discussing an employee's case with your legal advisers when you are considering disciplinary action or defending your organisation at an Employment Tribunal, for example.

All the disclosures discussed in this section are relatively rare, and the consequences of making a disclosure inappropriately could be serious. You should therefore consider setting up a formal procedure for considering all such disclosures, and approving them at a senior level. Keep a written record in the individual's file of what disclosure was made, to whom, and on what basis, together with any supporting evidence, and show clearly who authorised the disclosure.

If a 'crime and taxation' disclosure is deliberately made without the person's knowledge and they make a subject access request before they have become aware of the disclosure, the record of disclosure authorisation should not be shown to them; such information is specifically exempt from subject access if that would prejudice the purpose. Once they know the disclosure was made, or if their finding out would not matter, then they should be able to see the record of disclosure authorisation, because they have a legitimate interest in checking that the disclosure was properly made.

Normally, it is best to involve the police or other relevant authority as soon as you start to suspect that something is seriously wrong. Trying to investigate on your own carries all sorts of risks, including inadvertently invalidating potential evidence. The Information Commissioner does, however, provide benchmarks on data matching where it is used to identify possible fraud.

Information Commissioner's benchmarks on fraud detection

1   Consult Trade Unions or other worker representatives, if any, or workers themselves before starting a data matching exercise. Act on any legitimate concerns raised in consultation before starting the exercise.

2   Inform new workers of the use of payroll or other data in fraud prevention exercises and remind them of this periodically.

3   Do not disclose worker data to other organisations for the prevention or detection of fraud unless:

– you are required by law to make the disclosure, or

– you believe that failure to disclose, in a particular instance, is likely to prejudice the prevention or detection of crime, or

– the disclosure is provided for in workers' contracts of employment.

Raising the alert when you have concerns about an individual

What do you do if you are uneasy about a person's probity or suitability for particular work and then find that they are working with – or applying to work with – another organisation? Deciding whether to alert the other organisation or not can be a serious dilemma.

The question can arise in a range of circumstances, including:

■   protection of children or vulnerable adults;

■   financial probity – fraud or theft, for example;

■   unacceptable behaviour towards colleagues, including violence or harassment;

■   alcohol or drug misuse affecting work performance.

The key to the right behaviour must be the prevention of harm, as discussed in Chapter 3. Many investigations into specific tragedies discover that there was a trail of concerns, none of which had been shared, but which could have raised the alert in time. However, this does not mean that you can just say anything about anyone to anyone. Firstly, you need to be sure that the risk of harm is serious enough to warrant your interference; then you need to take the most appropriate action.

The question of the potential extent of harm is a matter of judgement. You may want to take into account the seriousness of your concern and the length of time that has elapsed. The principle behind the Rehabilitation of Offenders Act is that people can and do reform, and that past misdemeanours must not be used against someone who has genuinely changed their behaviour. At the same time, some offences are so serious that they never become 'spent' and some roles are so sensitive that offences have to be declared even if they are spent (see Appendix A).

Even where someone has done wrong in the past, that is not always a bar to them being employed or working as a volunteer. The organisation may decide that the context is sufficiently different, or that the person can be supervised closely enough, for the risk to be acceptably small in some roles. You should not automatically assume that someone's new employer is unaware of their past history.

Where official action has been taken against the individual in the past, this should show up in the course of a CRB check or in references. Your most important action, therefore, is to ensure that serious concerns are dealt with properly at the time and become a matter of record. This has the benefit of taking matters out of your hands, and also of making it more likely that other organisations will be warned, rather than leaving it to the chance of you coming across the person in their new role.

Don't be afraid to involve the police or other authorities, therefore, when things go wrong, or to take formal disciplinary action rather than just letting someone leave. Even if no further action is taken, for whatever reason, the fact that the police were called, or that the person was under investigation for a disciplinary offence when they walked out would be on the record. Of course, if the investigation is carried through and the person is exonerated this should also be put on record.

You *must* inform the authorities immediately about certain types of incident as soon as they occur, not when your internal procedures have run their course. For example:

- the Children's Homes Regulations 2001 say that you must inform the Care Standards Commission about 'any serious complaint about the home or persons working there';
- the Protection of Children Act 1999 says that a child care organisation *must* (and any other organisation *may*) tell the Department of Health, for possible inclusion on List 99 (see Glossary), not only when a child care worker is dismissed 'on the grounds of misconduct (whether or not in the course of his employment) which harmed a child or placed a child at risk of harm', but also when 'the individual has resigned or retired in circumstances such that the organisation would have dismissed him, or would have considered dismissing him, on such grounds if he had not resigned or retired';
- the Regulations on the Protection of Vulnerable Adults (POVA) say that registered persons have a duty to refer care workers for possible inclusion on

the POVA list where any action or inaction on the part of an individual has harmed a vulnerable adult or placed a vulnerable adult at risk of harm. Again, this applies not only when they are actually dismissed but when you could have dismissed them had they not resigned or retired.

Despite all these provisions, things may still go wrong.

■ Organisations may not report incidents which they should, or events may have happened before the current reporting arrangements were in place.

■ Devious individuals may change their name or other details and slip through the net.

■ Organisations may not carry out all the checks that they should, or may take an over-optimistic view of someone's rehabilitation.

■ Incidents that occur outside work when someone is already in post may not come to the organisation's notice. (For example someone working in a finance post may omit to tell their employer about their court appearance for defrauding the tennis club.) You may include in your contract a duty on the individual to own up, but even this does not guarantee that they will.

■ You may not have been asked for a reference because the individual knew that disadvantageous information would come to light.

You should treat each case seriously and individually and only take action after due consideration. If you decide, on balance, that you cannot remain silent, you still have to consider how to act. If you are convinced that there is a 'clear and present danger' there might well be a case for giving an immediate warning and dealing with any fallout afterwards. However, you must respect the rights of the individual too. If the danger is more diffuse, less urgent, or less serious, the best course of action might be to approach the individual, point out your concern and suggest that, if they have not already done so, they should own up to the other organisation.

If the person will not do so and you still have concerns, the other organisation should normally make their own decision, based on hard information. After all, they have to be satisfied that your concern is genuine. An organisation that penalised someone just on your say-so could be in big trouble if it turned out that the accusation was mistaken or malicious. You might, therefore, suggest to them that they should carry out a particular investigation or ask a particular set of questions.

One thing you must never do is to share CRB disclosures with other organisations. 'Unauthorised' disclosure of CRB information is an offence, and you cannot authorise a disclosure outside your organisation. The CRB Code explicitly says (in the appendix) that:

> *'a member, officer or employee of a body that is registered may only disclose Disclosure information:*
> - *in the course of his/ her duties, and*
> - *to another member, officer or employee of that body.'*

If you have CRB information about someone which gives you concern, the most you can do is suggest to the organisation using their services that they make a CRB check for themselves.

Where you have suspicions, but nothing has been fully investigated or proven, you may still feel sufficiently concerned that you do want to alert the other organisation. This, however, takes you into dangerous waters. If the information you are considering providing is not part of your organisation's records, but is merely information you hold in your head, the Data Protection Act would not apply. The decision on whether or not to say anything would be a matter for your careful judgement – remembering the risk of being sued for defamation if the information turns out to be wrong or impossible to substantiate.

If, however, you want to use material from your records, under the Data Protection Act your disclosure of such information would have to comply with all eight Principles. Here, the key one is probably the first, which says that your actions must be 'fair' as well as legal (which would include not being defamatory). Fairness normally means that the data subject should know what you are doing, unless there is a very good reason. So, again, the ideal situation might be to approach the individual and suggest that they clear matters up.

If they refuse, you might still argue that it was fair to disclose against their wishes, but you would have to meet one of the Schedule 2 'fair processing' Conditions. In some cases you could probably argue that you meet the sixth Condition (that it was in the 'legitimate interests' of the recipient organisation).

You would probably not want to disclose any 'sensitive' data (such as criminal record or alleged offences), because then you would have to meet one of the Schedule 3 Conditions. In some cases you could possibly argue the third of these (that it was 'necessary ... to protect the vital interests of the data subject or another person ... where ... consent ... has been unreasonably withheld'), but in order to meet this condition the danger would have to be significant and might even have to be in relation to specific people.

If you are in doubt about whether to raise a concern, it may be worth discussing the matter with an appropriate official agency, such as the police or CSCI, rather than going directly to another organisation.

Mergers and acquisitions

In the event that your organisation is involved in a merger, you are likely to have to exchange information about employees both during the negotiations and after the event. It is worth being aware of the Information Commissioner's guidance.

> **Information Commissioner's benchmarks on mergers and acquisitions**
>
> 1 Ensure, wherever practicable, that information handed over to another organisation in connection with a prospective acquisition or merger is anonymised.
>
> 2 Only hand over personal information prior to the final merger or acquisition decision after securing assurances that it will be used solely for the evaluation of assets and liabilities, it will be treated in confidence and will not be disclosed to other parties, and it will be destroyed or returned after use.
>
> 3 Advise workers wherever practicable if their employment records are to be disclosed to another organisation before an acquisition or merger takes place. If the acquisition or merger proceeds make sure workers are aware of the extent to which their records are to be transferred to the new employer.
>
> 4 Ensure that if you intend to disclose sensitive personal data a sensitive personal data condition is satisfied.
>
> 5 Where a merger or acquisition involves a transfer of information about a worker to a country outside the European Economic Area (EEA) ensure that there is a proper basis for making the transfer.
>
> 6 New employers should ensure that the records they hold as a result of a merger or acquisition do not include excessive information, and are accurate and relevant.

Chapter summary

Ensure that staff are aware of the types of disclosure (including publication) of their data that you make, both routine and exceptional.

Where there is no business requirement to insist on the disclosure, give staff the choice. In other cases enable staff to make representations if they have a reason for not wanting the disclosure or publication to be made.

Apply the above principles in the case of photographs. Where possible, allow staff to choose one image over another, even where a photograph must be disclosed or published.

Be clear with staff what kind of references you are prepared to provide and ensure that you have consent before disclosing sensitive data. Only give references in writing.

Staff must be given the opportunity to opt out of any use of their data for marketing, whether from within your organisation (in connection with fundraising, for example) or from outside.

Before releasing information to the police or other official bodies you must ensure that the disclosure is on a sound legal footing, in order to comply with the Data Protection Act.

There is usually nothing to stop you raising a concern about an individual with the appropriate body, especially where there is a risk of harm to others, but it is important to think it through, and act with fairness towards the individual.

chapter 14

EMPLOYMENT POLICIES AND PROCEDURES

At several points in this book we have suggested that it is important to have clear written statements setting out aspects of the relationship between your organisation and its staff. These may be benefits you provide which are outside the contract, such as training and development. They may be procedures your staff are expected to follow, aimed at delivering a good quality of service delivery or good-quality record-keeping. They may be standards of behaviour you expect from your staff – a breach of which would potentially result in disciplinary action.

With all of these, the purpose of having something in writing is so that everyone involved is clear about expectations, for themselves, for their colleagues and for the organisation they work for.

Many of the policies and procedures you may want to write down are a matter of choice or good practice, but some are mandatory. Under the CRB Code of Practice, for example, your organisation must have *written* policies covering:

- fair treatment in the employment of ex-offenders; and
- the correct handling and safe-keeping of disclosure information.

The various Care Standards Regulations also set out specific areas where you must have written policies if they apply to your organisation.

Even if there is no requirement to have a written policy, policies in key areas help to ensure consistency across the organisation, and can be very valuable in disciplinary cases. A written policy, and signed confirmation that on joining the organisation the employee read and understood it, provide solid evidence that the person knew (or should have known) they were doing wrong.

Most employment law specialists advise a clear separation of contractual and non-contractual material. This is because anything deemed contractual can only be varied if you follow a set legal process, which includes consultation with staff. This has two main consequences. The first is that your contract of employment should avoid references to policies which are not explicitly part of the contract. It should not say, for example, 'See absence policy' or 'See Acceptable Use Policy'.

The second is that all key statutory rights and any other provision that you want to make part of your contract must be summarised in the contract, not in the staff handbook. Any supporting procedures or additional information relating to statutory rights or contractual provisions may, and often should, be the subject of a separate policy.

Staff handbooks

Once you start accumulating policies to describe your expectations of staff, or the procedures they should follow in relation to their employment, it is common practice to assemble these into a staff handbook. Before embarking on a staff handbook you should consider seriously how it will be used and how you will keep it up-to-date. There are far too many cases of out of date handbooks languishing on high shelves or in the back of filing cabinets, with staff frequently unaware of what is in them.

If you feel that a handbook is likely to meet this fate in your organisation, and would therefore be a waste of resources, you may want to consider other options, such as these.

- Maintain one single copy of the handbook in the personnel department, where it can be consulted by all staff. Notify all staff by e-mail or memo when significant details change (but save up a number of changes and make them all at once, rather than issuing daily notices of small changes).
- Place all the documents that would be in a handbook on an 'intranet' or private area of the organisation's web site, where they can be viewed by all staff. Remind staff from time to time where to find the documents.
- Maintain compliance with your policies by reminding staff about them at staff meetings, training and refresher sessions rather than by distributing detailed procedural documents.
- Simplify your policies so that staff are more likely to remember what they say without having to consult the full policy.

A staff handbook must be kept up-to-date, but must not be totally fluid. It is important to be able to tell exactly what policy was in force at any given time. You should therefore have a proper change management procedure, which ensures that changes to any section of the handbook are properly approved, with a specific start date, and that all relevant staff are notified when policies or procedures are changed.

This book is not the place to go into detail about the content of your policies. Guidance on this can be found among the resources in Chapter 18. However, if you do decide to produce and maintain a staff handbook or comprehensive staff web site, you may want to consider the contents list given in Appendix M, which is based on the handbook of a large, national care organisation with dispersed sites:

Chapter summary

You are likely to find the need for written policies in a variety of areas. It may be convenient to collect these in a staff handbook, but there are alternative ways of making them available.

Material which is part of your contract must be clearly identified, and may not be appropriate to include in the staff handbook.

Document	Main requirements	Retention period	File location
Staff handbook	Contractual polices and procedures may be referred to, but the contractual details must be established separately from the handbook	Date each version of each policy carefully and keep for 6 years after it has been superseded	Personnel department

chapter 15

LEAVING THE ORGANISATION

When someone leaves your organisation, the main concerns over your records will be as follows.

- Accurately recording the circumstances and timing of the individual's departure.
- Ensuring that your records are completely up-to-date and accurate so that you can finalise any outstanding financial arrangements – such as overtime pay, pay in lieu of holidays not yet taken, or outstanding loans.
- Notifying all relevant staff of their departure, so that their computer access can be cancelled, internal telephone directories updated, keys, equipment and other organisational property recovered and so on, and recording that this has been done, if necessary.
- Notifying the relevant authorities, where this is required, if the person is dismissed for certain types of misconduct.
- Recording any information you need from the individual, such as handing-over notes for their successor, any suggestions about the job description of their replacement, or the outcome of an exit interview, if you carry these out.
- Agreeing with the individual, if necessary, the scope of any references you will provide for them in future.
- Deciding (partly in the light of the above) which information from their file you will keep, and how long for.

Just as you would have an induction record, it may be worth considering a departure checklist to ensure that you do not overlook anything (see Appendix O).

Don't forget that if someone leaves your organisation because you have dismissed them for inappropriate conduct, or when you were about to investigate conduct which could have led to dismissal, you must consider whether you need to report them to the Department of Health. You may have a statutory duty to do this, or it may be at your discretion, depending on what type of service you provide. (See Chapter 13 for a more detailed discussion.)

Retention and archiving

After someone has left your organisation you will want to carry out the minimum possible amount of work on their file in future. As discussed in Chapter 6, with good planning the file may only need reviewing once or twice before archiving. A possible approach is therefore to divide the contents of their file immediately into three, or possibly four, categories.

- All the material that will be disposed of after six months, or as soon as you are sure that there are no loose ends to tie up (whichever is later). This could include surplus copies of material where one copy will be held for longer.
- Optionally, a set of material that will be kept for three or four years. If this does not amount to much, and there is no risk to the individual in holding it, there is probably a case for amalgamating this category with the following one.
- A set of material that will be kept for six or seven years.
- A small amount of material that will be kept indefinitely.

When the relevant review period arrives, there is then no need to examine the file; it is just a matter of removing the next, pre-sorted, batch of material for destruction.

When material is to be disposed of, don't forget to ensure that all copies of the information are destroyed. You may, for example, have both electronic and paper versions of some information, which should normally both be disposed of at the same time.

Specific retention periods are set in the various Care Standards regulations (see under 'Information for service providers' on the CSCI web site given in the Resources section on page 184). These can require more information to be kept, for much longer, than in other types of work. If you are subject to any of these regulations you must check the relevant regulations carefully and apply the time limits appropriate to your schedule. If your work involves children or vulnerable adults but you are not subject to any regulations it may be appropriate for you to consider holding information for equivalent lengths of time.

Although there is a lot of common ground, there are subtle differences between the different regulations. For example, the regulations for children's homes (SI 2001 No. 3967) say that specified records 'shall be retained for at least 15 years from the date of the last entry ...'. The specified records include, among others, basic details of everyone who has ever worked at the home and also 'a copy of the staff duty roster of persons working at the children's home, and a record of the actual rosters worked.' The regulations for care homes (SI 2001 No. 3965) contain similar provisions, but instead of just basic details of people employed at the home specify also 'correspondence, reports, records of disciplinary action and any other records in relation to his employment'. However, they only specify a three year retention period.

This book cannot set out the detailed requirements, and before setting your retention periods you must look at the Care Standards Regulations which apply to you, or to the type of work which is closest to yours.

> **Information Commissioner's benchmarks on retention of records**
>
> 1 Establish and adhere to standard retention times for categories of information held on the records of workers and former workers. Base the retention times on business need taking into account relevant professional guidelines.
> 2 Anonymise any data about workers and former workers where practicable.
> 3 If the holding of any information on criminal convictions of workers is justified, ensure that the information is deleted once the conviction is 'spent' under the Rehabilitation of Offenders Act.
> 4 Ensure that records which are to be disposed of are securely and effectively destroyed.

Chapter summary

You may want to use a leaving checklist to ensure that nothing is overlooked when a member of staff leaves your organisation.

You should aim to divide your personnel records into three or four categories when someone leaves.

- That which is kept only while loose ends are tied up.
- That which is kept for three to four years.
- That which is kept for six to seven years.
- That which is kept indefinitely.

It may be appropriate to combine the middle two categories and keep for six to seven years. Retention periods for certain information may be significantly longer if your activities are subject to Care Standards.

Document	Main requirements	Retention period	File location
Leaver's checklist	Complete and accurate	6 years	Personnel file

chapter 16

OVERSEAS WORKERS

Some voluntary organisations employ people to work overseas, while others send workers who are based in the UK overseas from time to time.

The main considerations from the record-keeping point of view are:

- if someone is employed to work overseas you must ensure that you keep any records which are required by the country they work in, as well as any required for the UK;
- if you transfer information from your records to countries outside the UK, you must ensure that there is no breach of Data Protection.

This book cannot attempt to go into the kind of records which might be required overseas, although it has to be said that good quality records which are fit for your purposes in this country are likely to meet at least a large majority of the requirements elsewhere.

The eighth Data Protection Principle, on the face of it, prohibits the transfer of personal data overseas unless it remains protected by law. Schedule 4 of the Act, however, provides for cases in which this provision can be over-ridden. The three most relevant here are:

- where a contract between you and the recipient organisation guarantees that the data will be protected;
- where the transfer is necessary for a contract between you and the individual;
- where you have the consent of the individual.

Protection by law

Protection by law is automatically available in all countries of the European Economic Area (EEA). Note that the Channel Islands and the Isle of Man are not in the EEA, but they have legislation in place (or in the case of Jersey soon will have legislation in place) which has been approved by the European Commission (EC) as have Switzerland and Argentina.

A scheme has also been negotiated with the United States of America whereby recipient organisations in that country can sign up to the 'safe harbors' provisions, which are deemed to provide the same level of protection. (This has not proved a very popular arrangement, so it is quite likely that organisations you are dealing with in the USA will not have signed up, or even heard of it.)

Protection by contract with the recipient

If you want to protect the information by a contract between you and the recipient organisation, this must be in a form approved by the EC. At the time of writing new provisions had just been released, revising the approved form of contract in the light of experience; you should check with the Information Commissioner for guidance in this area.

Transfer where the data is unprotected

Although it is better to maintain protection, either by law or by contract, when data is transferred, this is not always possible. The risk of transferring data where it is not protected may be outweighed by the need to get on with the job, or may be felt acceptable by the individual.

There are many cases where you will be able to argue that the transfer of information is necessary for the contract between you and the individual. For example, if someone is employed in a role which involves them travelling or working overseas, you are very likely to have to pass details about them to their contacts in other countries. You will also have to give their details to travel companies, airlines, hotels and possibly government authorities. The key consideration here is that the transfer of information must be *necessary* for the contract. You have to make the case either that they couldn't do their work or that you couldn't meet your obligations to them without the transfer.

If you cannot show that the transfer is necessary, it is still permissible to make it if the individual gives their consent – remembering that consent must be 'specific, informed and freely given'.

In order to meet the 'transparency' requirements in the first Data Protection principle, the individual must know what types of information you are intending to transfer overseas, even if you are not giving them any choice in the matter. If they know what is happening they may be able to alert you to potential harm that you had not identified, either in relation to particular types of data or the country it is going to or the intended recipient.

Where data is being transferred without protection, it obviously makes sense to be particularly careful to transfer only the minimum amount necessary.

Chapter summary

If you transfer information about your staff overseas you must ensure that either:

■ the data remains protected by law or by contract with the recipient, or

■ the loss of protection is justified by your business necessity or by the consent of the individual.

In effect, for most of Europe there are no special considerations involved in transferring data about your staff. Outside Europe the key is to make sure they know what you are doing, or better still proposing to do, so that they can raise any concerns with you before it is too late.

VOLUNTEERS

Good record-keeping is just as essential in the case of volunteers as for paid staff, not least because of the increasing importance of vetting, and of being able to demonstrate how quality standards are maintained in a service delivered partly or largely by volunteers. However, the key difference with volunteers is that there is no contract of employment between you and them. Your record-keeping must demonstrate this; if there is any suggestion of arrangements between you and the volunteers which might be construed as a contract, even if you did not intend it, this could have very serious consequences. This chapter briefly examines the similarities and differences between employee and volunteer record-keeping, following broadly the same order as the chapters in the book.

Data Protection, subject access to files and disclosure of information

You should also consult Chapters 3, 7 and 13 in this book for the background to these issues.

Volunteers are data subjects in exactly the same way as paid staff. They have the same rights, including:

- to know what their information is being used for and who it might be passed on to;
- to have it treated confidentially;
- to have it kept accurate and up-to-date;
- to be given a choice over how it is being used, where this is possible (or required, in the case of marketing); and
- to have access to the information held about them.

An open files policy is just as relevant with volunteers as with paid staff.

The same principles also apply to disclosures of information. Normally you would expect to make volunteers aware of how and when information about them would be disclosed, and to get consent in out-of-the-ordinary situations. Where there is a risk to other people, exactly the same considerations would apply as those discussed for paid staff – with the same caveats that if you do decide that you need to disclose a concern, you must ensure that you go about it in the right way.

Where you are obliged (or invited) to report misconduct against children or vulnerable adults in respect of staff, the same provision normally applies to volunteers.

General considerations

You should also consult Chapters 4 and 5 in this book for the background to these issues.

The 'owner' of your volunteer records may be a volunteer organiser rather than the personnel department. It is worth liaising between the two, however, to ensure that the two sets of records are handled consistently and that very similar procedures are followed in terms of how you store them and how you maintain confidentiality and security.

Many of your volunteer records would mirror quite closely the equivalent part of the employee's personnel files.

- Basic contact and other material would usually be almost identical.
- Payroll and financial records would normally be limited to expenses claims, but would probably still be handled by the finance department.
- Records of CRB checks are just as important with volunteers as with paid staff, but you would not need to make the same checks on their right to work. (Even asylum seekers whose documents state that they are not allowed to do any work, paid or unpaid, are allowed to volunteer and receive expenses. See the Volunteering England web site given in the Resources section on page 190.)
- Induction, training, supervision and appraisal records might not have the same content, but it is important that volunteers are properly inducted, trained and supervised and that you record this appropriately.
- Records of file access should be kept in the same way as for employees.
- Miscellaneous material should also be kept in the same way.

Recruitment and selection

You should also consult Chapter 8 in this book for the principles that would apply to volunteer recruitment and selection records. Make sure, however, that your procedures distinguish between recruitment of employees with whom you will have an employment contract, and volunteers.

It is just as important to match the right volunteer to the right opportunity as it is to match the right employee to the right job. You should therefore have a recruitment and selection process to ensure this.

The content of the documentation may very well be much less complex and detailed. Nevertheless you are likely to have equivalents to the job description, person specification, application form and interview notes. You are also likely to have to verify key parts of the information provided and carry out any necessary CRB checks.

In all of this you should consider modelling your approach on that set out in Chapter 8, making the necessary changes to reflect the different needs in volunteer posts.

Volunteer agreements

With volunteers you must be careful not to enter a contract when you don't mean to. On the one hand you want to give volunteers the security of knowing what treatment they can expect. You may also want to set out the expectations you have of them. If you are depending on volunteers to provide a service, you need them to be reliable and effective. On the other hand, you must not turn them into employees by mistake. They would then be entitled to pay (at the minimum wage or higher) and all the other benefits and rights of employment.

Many organisations offer volunteers a non-contractual agreement. Any agreement you do enter into must talk about intentions, expectations and privileges. If you mention rights, obligations, sick leave, annual leave, contract, terms and conditions, disciplinary procedures, or any other provision normally found in a contract you might find yourself with employees instead of volunteers – an expensive mistake. You must also make it plain that the agreement is binding 'in honour only' and is not intended to be legally binding.

A list of what to include in a volunteer agreement can be found in the *Voluntary Sector Legal Handbook*, and also on the web site of Volunteering England (see the Resources section page 184 and 190 respectively). The precise definition of volunteers and their status is complex and there have been several attempts to obtain specific employment rights for volunteers at tribunals (for example a case in early 2005 alleging the right of volunteers to claim unfair dismissal). For the latest case law see Sandy Adirondack's web site or Volunteering England (see the Resources section on pages 182 and 190 respectively).

Leave, sickness absence and health

You should also consult Chapter 11 in this book for a discussion of the issues surrounding health information.

For volunteers, of course, there is no pay issue when they are not at work. However, there are good management reasons for needing to know when they are (or are not) going to be available, how much time they have worked, and how regularly each volunteer is able to attend.

You should ask for advance notice of a volunteer being unable to come to work, wherever possible, to help you plan around the volunteer's absence. However, you should be wary of *requiring* volunteers to notify you, because of the potential for creating a contract unintentionally through 'mutuality of obligation'.

For this reason your forms for notifying and recording times when the volunteer will not be available (or did not turn up) should be different from those for employees, and require just the minimum information.

Where a volunteer is away because of illness you may feel that you need to satisfy yourself that the work did not contribute to it; you do have health and safety responsibilities to your volunteers. Your volunteers may also have health problems or disabilities which prevent them getting paid work; you may need to record these so that you can support the volunteers appropriately and ensure that you do not ask them to do work they are not up to.

Since health information is 'sensitive', you are likely to need the individual's 'explicit' consent – normally indicated by a signature – in order to hold it. In many cases it will be appropriate to leave the decision to them on whether you can hold the information or not. Where there are health and safety considerations, or other over-riding reasons for you needing to know about the health of volunteers, you may want to specify that you are unable to take someone on as a volunteer who does not consent to you obtaining and using information about their health. If you do this you should be particularly careful about proportionality, only holding information that you can absolute justify.

Volunteer handbooks

A volunteer handbook should contain just those standard policies and procedures in your organisation that apply to volunteers – on confidentiality, or on smoking, for example – along with other relevant material, such as that concerned with what expenses can be claimed back and how to claim them.

It is not good practice to issue volunteers with your staff handbook, as this will probably refer to procedures connected with contractual rights and it is vital not to confuse volunteers with employees.

Retention periods

You should also consult Chapter 6 in this book for further details.

Volunteers cannot make many of the claims for unfair treatment or breach of contract which lie behind the sometimes lengthy retention periods for employee records. You may therefore decide that you will keep some of the records for less time. The chapter summary looks at the possible implications of this.

The Care Standards Act 2000 and its related Regulations requires you in some cases to keep records about volunteers who have worked for you at similar levels of detail and for the same amount of time as those of paid staff.

Chapter summary

Volunteer records should be treated in the same way as those of paid staff, although the content will in some areas be very different and the file as a whole may be less complex.

Retention periods for volunteer records may be shorter than those for paid staff, except where Care Standards apply. The table below excludes Care Standards considerations.

Document	Main requirements	Retention period	File location
Volunteer agreement	Must not amount to a contract of employment	While the volunteer is working for you	On volunteer record
Contact and other details	Must be up-to-date	While the volunteer is working for you	On volunteer record
Expenses records	Accuracy	3 years (in most cases)	In accounts system
Records of CRB and other checks	Legal compliance	See Chapter 8	Normally held separately in personnel department
Holidays and sickness absence records	Beware of requiring attendance	While the volunteer is working for you	On volunteer record
Induction, training, supervision and appraisal records	Agreed with individual	While the volunteer is working for you	On volunteer record
Records of file access	Honest and complete	While file exists	On volunteer record
Miscellaneous material	Must be relevant	While relevant	On volunteer record

chapter 18

RESOURCES

Employment law changes continually, and best practice evolves. In most cases the most up-to-date information can be found on the web, and you should always try to check the latest position on one or more of the web sites given below (whose addresses have been checked during January 2005).

Books can give a different perspective, and those on best practice do not go out of date so quickly. We have generally not listed shorter publications here, since many of these are most easily acquired, often at no cost, through the relevant web site. However, all publications which have been explicitly drawn on in preparing this book are included.

Sources of books and legislation

Many of the books listed are available from:

Directory of Social Change
Tel: 08450 77 77 07
Web site: www.dsc.org.uk/acatalog/catalogbody.html

Acts of Parliament (from 1988 onwards) and **Statutory Instruments** (from 1987 onwards)
Available free of charge on-line from:

> **Her Majesty's Stationery Office (HMSO)**
> Web site: www.hmso.gov.uk
> To find Acts quickly, you need to know the year; they are then listed alphabetically. For Statutory Instruments it is best to know the year and number, although it is also possible to search by name.
> Printed copies of legislation can be bought from some bookshops or:
> **The Stationery Office (TSO)**
> Web site: www.tso.co.uk/bookshop
> PO Box 29, St Crispins, Duke Street, Norwich NR3 1GN
> Tel: 0870 600 5522 Fax: 0870 600 5533

Web sites referred to in this book rarely specify whether the information they contain applies throughout the UK or only to specific parts. While in many cases good practice remains the same, readers in Scotland, Wales and Northern Ireland should check for the detailed legal position.

Information on Scottish legislation and policies is available from the Scottish Council for Voluntary Organisations (www.scvo.org.uk) or the Scottish Executive (www.scotland.gov.uk).

Information on Welsh legislation and policies is available from the Wales Council for Voluntary Action (www.wcva.org.uk) or the Welsh Assembly (www.wales.gov.uk).

Information on Northern Irish legislation and policies is available from the Northern Ireland Council for Voluntary Action (www.nicva.org) or Online Northern Ireland (www.onlineni.net) and, particularly on employment matters, the Department for Employment and Learning Northern Ireland (www.delni.gov.uk).

See also Appendix A for more on the legal background.

General resources on employment law and good practice

Acas
Helpline: 08457 47 47 47
Web site: www.acas.org.uk

(Originally the Advisory, Conciliation and Arbitration Service.) Provides helpful guidance on most areas, not just discipline and dismissal, along with model policies and procedures and a wide variety of sample forms. Acas also has regional offices and a range of other services for employers.

Sandy Adirondack
Web site: www.sandy-a.co.uk/employment.htm

Detailed updates on employment issues affecting the voluntary sector.

CIPD
Tel: 020 8971 9000
Web site: www.cipd.co.uk

The Chartered Institute for Personnel and Development. Detailed information, advice line and other resources, but mostly available only to members.

Labour Research Department
Web site: www.lrd.org.uk

A range of paid-for publications and other services, aimed at trade unionists, but relevant for good practice.

Department of Trade and Industry
Web site: www.dti.gov.uk

> Covers the law and gives guidance on all areas of employment, in the section 'For employees'.

Trade Union Congress
Web site: www.tuc.org.uk

> Free of charge information on employment rights, welfare, etc.

WorkSmart
Web site: www.worksmart.org.uk/rights/index.php

> TUC service explaining employment rights, etc.

Employment Law Handbook   Daniel Barnet and Henry Scrope
The Law Society, 2004, ISBN 1 85328 970 1

> One of the more accessible standard reference works.

Just About Managing?   Sandy Adirondack
London Voluntary Service Council, 3rd ed 1998, ISBN 1 872582 17 6

> User-friendly guide and reference book for managers and management committees of small and medium-sized voluntary and community organisations.

Management shapers series from CIPD (see above)

> A series of small books on key topics such as *Appraisal Interviewing* and *Assertiveness*, but particularly good is *Asking Questions* by Ian Mackay, ISBN 0 85292 768 1
> Full list from www.cipdpublishing.co.uk

Managing Conflict   Gill Taylor
Directory of Social Change, 1999, ISBN 1 900360 28 4

> Techniques for understanding and resolving conflict at work and in employment situations.

Managing People   Gill Taylor and Christine Thornton
Directory of Social Change, 1995, ISBN 1 873860 47 1

> Scenario-based discussion of challenges faced by voluntary sector managers.

Voluntary but not Amateur   Ruth Hayes and Jacki Reason
London Voluntary Service Council, 7th ed 2004, ISBN 1 872582 32 X

> A guide to the law for voluntary organisations and community groups, with sections on recruitment and employment.

The Voluntary Sector Legal Handbook Sandy Adirondack and James Sinclair Taylor

Directory of Social Change, 2nd edition 2001, ISBN 1 900360 72 1

> A 900-page guide to all aspects of the law affecting voluntary organisations, including employment and the management of volunteers. Details of changes since publication can be found at www.sandy-a.co.uk/vslh.htm.

Criminal records checks, right to work and Care Standards

Care Standards Inspectorate for Wales

Tel: 02920 825111

Web site: www.csiw.wales.gov.uk

> An independent part of the National Assembly for Wales, which regulates social care, early years and private and voluntary health care services in Wales.

CSCI (Commission for Social Care Inspection)

Helpline: 0845 015 0120

Web site: www.csci.gov.uk

> The inspectorate for all social care services in England. The 'Information for service providers' on the web site contains extensive information on the law, including regulations and national minimum standards, and the inspection process.

CRB (Criminal Records Bureau)

Helpline: 0870 90 90 811

Web site: www.crb.gov.uk

> Agency providing disclosure of criminal records and other information which might prevent people from working in certain types of job. Under 'Publications' are sub-sections: Publications, which includes the *CRB Code of Practice and Explanatory Guide*; and Guidance, which includes the NACRO guide on the employment of ex-offenders (see below).

Disclosure service

Web site: www.disclosure.gov.uk

> CRB web site specifically dealing with the process of disclosure. The CRB *Code of Practice* can be downloaded from here, as well as publications such as CRB guidance notes and *Employing Ex Offenders: A Practical Guide* produced by the CIPD (see above).

Disclosure Scotland

Web site: www.disclosurescotland.co.uk

The separate disclosure service for Scotland.

Home Office

Employer's helpline: 0845 010 6677

Web site: www.homeoffice.gov.uk

Information on immigration and nationality, and right to work. See 'Comprehensive guidance for UK employers on preventing illegal working' (follow links to immigration and nationality and then prevention of illegal working).

NACRO

Tel: 020 7582 6500

Web site: www.nacro.org.uk

An organisation that works with ex offenders and promotes good practice in employment and other areas. See for example, *Recruiting Ex-offenders: the Employers' Perspective*, ISBN 0 85069 194 X

Northern Ireland Social Services Inspectorate

Tel: 0289 0520500

Web site: www.dhsspsni.gov.uk/hss/ssi/index.asp

Formerly the Northern Ireland Department of Health, Social Services and Public Safety – Social Services Inspectorate.

Scottish Commission for Regulation of Care

Tel: 01382 207100

Web site: www.carecommission.com

Also known as The Care Commission. Regulates and inspects Scottish care services.

Data Protection (including the right of access)

Department for Constitutional Affairs

Web site: www.dca.gov.uk

The government department with responsibility for policy on Data Protection, Freedom of Information and related areas. For Data Protection see under 'People's rights'.

Information Commissioner

Tel: 01625 545700

Web site: www.informationcommissioner.gov.uk

The agency responsible for overseeing the practical implementation of Data Protection, Freedom of Information and related areas. See 'Data Protection' then 'Your legal obligations'. The Commissioner's *Code of Practice* on employment records – all four parts, plus various summaries and supplementary information – can then be found under 'Codes of practice'. The Commissioner's *Notification Handbook: A Complete Guide to Notification*, is available free by post or download.

Telephone Helplines Association

Web site: www.helplines.org.uk

Has published information on interception of telephone calls.

Data Protection for Voluntary Organisations Paul Ticher

Directory of Social Change, 2nd edition 2002, ISBN 1 903991 19 6

All aspects of Data Protection, concentrating on issues relevant to voluntary organisations, and with numerous examples to clarify areas of confusion.

Discrimination and equality

Commission for Racial Equality

Tel: 020 7939 0000 (also regional offices)

Web site: www.cre.gov.uk

Promotes good practice in employment and service provision. The web site has briefings covering key areas (such as employment and ethnic monitoring), and a comprehensive publications list, some available for free download.

Disability Rights Commission

Helpline: 08457 622 633

Web site: www.drc-gb.org

Promotes good practice in employment and service provision. The web site has a section on employment and a list of publications available for free download. Among these is a *Code of Practice* which is available on-line only.

Equality Direct

Helpline: 0845 600 3444

Web site: www.equalitydirect.org.uk

A confidential telephone helpline designed to 'give business managers easy access to authoritative and joined-up advice on a wide range of equality issues'.

Equal Opportunities Commission
Helpline: 0845 601 5901
Web site: www.eoc.org.uk

Promotes good practice in employment and service provision. The web site has detailed guidance on equal pay, equal treatment and family-friendly working, as well as a section giving the legal background.

Harassment Law
Web site: www.harassment-law.co.uk

Aimed at victims of harassment, rather than employers, but has some useful background information and links.

Job Centre Plus
Web site: www.jobcentreplus.gov.uk

Mainly concerned with recruitment and getting people into work. The Employer's home page has a link to disability services and the Disability Symbol.

Stonewall
Web site: www.stonewall.org.uk

Campaign for equality and justice for lesbians, gay men and bisexuals. A briefing for employees and a guide for employers are available for free download.

Discrimination Law Handbook Gill Palmer *et al.*
Legal Action Group, 2002, ISBN 1 903307 13 9

Ethnic Monitoring: A Guide for Public Authorities
CRE, 2002, ISBN 1 85442 434 3

Explains the main principles of ethnic monitoring in detail, focusing on employment and service delivery.

Electronic personnel records systems

Lasa (London Advice Services Alliance)
Web site: www.lasa.org.uk

Provides, among other things, information and other resources on information technology, including database development.

National Council for Voluntary Organisations
Web site: www.ncvo-vol.org.uk
Helpdesk: 0800 2 798 798

Offers a free helpdesk to anyone in the voluntary sector, on topics that include personnel issues and information technology.

Software source
Web site: www.softwaresource.co.uk

'The independent guide to HR products and services produced by *People Management*.' The database lists hundreds of software suppliers providing products with a role of some kind in human resources.

Health and safety

Health and Safety Executive
Web site: www.hse.gov.uk
Information line: 08701 545 500

Guidance and information on all aspects of health and safety. The web site includes a facility to report accidents on-line.

Accident book BI 510
Health and Safety Executive, May 2003, ISBN 0 7176 2603 2

Redesigned to be compliant with Data Protection.

Pay, pensions, tax, benefits and family-related leave

Inland Revenue
Employer's helpline: 08457 143 143 (one of a number of specific helplines)
Web site: www.inlandrevenue.gov.uk

Covers topics such as tax, National Insurance and related benefits. Includes details of how to operate SSP and SMP and offers downloadable official forms, including self-certification forms.

Maternity Alliance
Web site: www.maternityalliance.org.uk

> A national charity working to improve rights and services for pregnant women, new parents and their families. Web site provides information on employment rights and benefits.

OPAS (Pensions Advisory Service)
Helpline: 0845 601 2923
Web site: www.opas.org.uk

> 'An independent non-profit organisation that provides information and guidance on the whole spectrum of pensions covering State, company, personal and stakeholder schemes.'

TIGER
Web site: www.tiger.gov.uk

> (Tailored Interactive Guide on Employment Rights.) Interactive part of the Acas site, dealing with rights concerning maternity, paternity, adoptions, flexible working and the national minimum wage.

Department of Work and Pensions
Web site: www.dwp.gov.uk

> Information on benefits such as SSP (also in leaflet NI268); select the topic from the Benefits and Services A–Z.

Performance management

Managing Absence   Sarah Hargreaves, Christina Morton and Gill Taylor
Russell House Publishing, 1998, ISBN 1 898924 17 1

> Covers good practice and the basics of the legal position.

Managing Discipline and Dismissal   Gill Taylor
Directory of Social Change, forthcoming

Managing Dismissals   Daniel Barnett
Tolleys, 2nd ed. 2004, ISBN 0 7545 2213 X

Recruitment and selection

Managing Recruitment and Selection   Gill Taylor
Directory of Social Change, 1996, ISBN 1 873860 85 4

> Scenario-based coverage of good practice and many recruitment and selection issues, including job descriptions and person specifications.

Retention periods and records management

The National Archives
Web site: www.nationalarchives.gov.uk

> Although the National Archives (previously the Public Record Office) is mainly concerned with the care of government documents and making them available to the public, it also gives some guidance – aimed largely at government departments – on 'Records management'. This provides useful background, although much of the detail is unlikely to apply to most voluntary organisations.

Volunteers

Volunteering England
Tel: 0845 305 6979
Web site: www.volunteering.org.uk

> The national umbrella body on all aspects of volunteering. The web site has a section on 'Managing volunteers', with a few free guides and a more extensive list of paid-for publications.

Essential Volunteer Management   Steve McCurley and Rick Lynch
Directory of Social Change, 2nd ed. 1998 ISBN 1 900360 18 7

> Covers all aspects of recruiting and managing volunteers.

APPENDICES

APPENDICES

Appendix A: Relevant legislation

This book generally relates to the law as it applies in England. Much of the law applicable in Wales, Scotland and Northern Ireland is the same or similar, but this is not always the case. There are different care inspection regimes in each part of the UK, for example.

The main UK legislation is set out in Acts of Parliament, or 'Acts'. Details of the legislation are often not in the Acts themselves, but in subordinate Orders or Regulations which are collectively known as Statutory Instruments. This is generally done because Statutory Instruments are easier to bring in and to change, giving greater flexibility. Acts and Statutory Instruments may apply to the whole of the UK equally, to the whole of the UK but with local variations, or only to a specific part or parts of the UK.

Scotland has always had significant legal differences from England. UK Acts and Statutory Instruments often have to provide for this and, in addition, the Scottish Parliament now has its own power to legislate on certain 'devolved' matters.

For Wales most legislation is the same as in England, but the National Assembly for Wales has devolved powers to make some changes.

For Northern Ireland, special provision frequently has to be made in UK legislation, since the institutions are generally different, and some law is also different – on discrimination for example. The Northern Ireland Assembly has devolved powers, although at the time of writing these are suspended.

Discrimination

Key legislation includes:

- Sex Discrimination Act 1975 and Sex Discrimination (NI) Order 1976 and amendment
- Race Relations Act 1976 and Race Relations Amendments Act 2000.
- Fair Employment (NI) Acts 1989 and Fair Employment Monitoring Regulations (NI) 1989
- Disability Discrimination Act 1995 and Disability Discrimination Act 1995 (Amendment) Regulations 2003
- Employment Equality (Sexual Orientation) Regulations 2003
- Employment Equality (Religion or Belief) Regulations 2003

These Acts define areas of direct and indirect discrimination and victimisation, and set positive action measures for: people of different ethnic and racial groups, women, married people, men, people of different sexual orientation and people of different religions or beliefs (and in Northern Ireland different political beliefs).

The 'Dekker' decision of the European Court of Justice makes it unlawful to discriminate against pregnant women in the selection process.

The Equal Pay Act 1970 says that you cannot pay men and women doing the same job, or jobs of equal value, differently on grounds of gender alone.

Union membership

The Trade Union and Labour Relations (Consolidation) Act 1992 makes it illegal to discriminate against people on the basis of whether or not they are members of a trade union.

Rehabilitation of offenders

- Rehabilitation of Offenders Act 1974 and Exceptions Order 1975
- Rehabilitation of Offenders (NI) Order 1978 and Exceptions Order 1979

This legislation allows offenders who have a 'spent' sentence not to declare it when applying for a job unless the job is in one of the exempt categories.

The following table shows some of the key rehabilitation periods at the time of writing. Note that this legislation is under review. For the latest position, more detail on a wider range of sentence types, and an explanation of how reoffending and other matters are treated, see the NACRO publication on the CRB web site at www.crb.gov.uk/downloads/Recruiting_ex-offenders.pdf

Sentence	Rehabilitation period for people aged under 18 when convicted	Rehabilitation period for people aged 18 or over when convicted
Prison sentences[1] of 6 months or less	3 years	7 years
Prison sentences[1] of more than 6 months to 2 years	5 years	10 years
Fines[2], compensation, probation[3], community service[4], combination[5], action plan, curfew, drug treatment and testing, and reparation orders	2 years	5 years
Absolute discharge	6 months	6 months

[1] Including suspended sentences, youth custody (abolished in 1988) and detention in a young offender institution (abolished for under 18 year olds in 2000 and for those aged 18-20 in 2001).
[2] Even if subsequently imprisoned for fine default.
[3] For people convicted on or after 3 February 1995. These orders are now called community rehabilitation orders.
[4] These orders are now called community punishment orders.
[5] These orders are now called community punishment and rehabilitation orders.

Source: adapted from the NACRO publication Recruiting Ex-offenders: the Employer's Perspective.

If a job is exempt from the rehabilitation of offenders provisions, 'spent' convictions must be disclosed. Your application form must state this.

Exemptions are specified in terms of professions, offices and employments, and regulated occupations.

Exempt professions (in full):

- Actuary
- Any profession to which the Professions Supplementary to Medicine Act 1960 applies and which is undertaken following registration under that Act
- Barrister (in England and Wales), advocate (in Scotland), solicitor
- Chartered accountant, certified accountant
- Chartered psychologist
- Dentist, dental hygienist, dental auxiliary
- Legal executive
- Medical practitioner
- Nurse, midwife
- Ophthalmic optician, dispensing optician
- Pharmaceutical chemist
- Receiver appointed by the Court of Protection
- Registered chiropractor
- Registered foreign lawyer
- Registered osteopath
- Registered teacher (in Scotland)
- Veterinary surgeon

Exempt offices and employments which are likely to be relevant to voluntary organisations include:

- any employment in the Royal Society for the Prevention of Cruelty to Animals where the person employed or working, as part of their duties, may carry out the killing of animals;
- any employment or other work which is concerned with the provision of health services and which is of such a kind as to enable the holder of that employment or the person engaged in that work to have access to persons in receipt of such services in the course of their normal duties;
- any employment which is concerned with the administration of, or is otherwise normally carried out wholly or partly within the precincts of, a prison, remand centre, detention centre, or young offenders institution, and members of boards of visitors appointed under section 6 of the Prison Act 1952 or of visiting committees appointed under section 7 of the Prisons (Scotland) Act 1952;

- any employment which is concerned with the monitoring, for the purposes of child protection, of communications by means of the internet;
- any work which is (a) work in a regulated position; or (b) work in a further education institution where the normal duties of that work involve regular contact with persons aged under 18.

Further exempt offices and employments not shown above are largely connected with the police, the legal system or tax collection.

Exempt regulated occupations (in full).

- Any occupation in respect of which an application to the Gaming Board for Great Britain for a licence, certificate or registration is required by or under any enactment.
- Any occupation in respect of which the holder, as occupier of premises on which explosives are kept, is required by any Order of Council made under section 43 of the Explosives Act 1875 to obtain from the police or a court of summary jurisdiction a certificate as to his or her fitness to keep the explosives.
- Any occupation which is concerned with carrying on an establishment in respect of which registration is required by section 37 of the National Assistance Act 1948 or section 61 of the Social Work (Scotland) Act 1968.
- Any occupation which is concerned with:
  - the management of a place in respect of which the approval of the Secretary of State is required by section 1 of the Abortion Act 1967.
  - in England and Wales, carrying on a nursing home in respect of which registration is required by section 187 of the Public Health Act 1936 or section 14.
  - in Scotland, carrying on a nursing home in respect of which registration is required under section 1 of the Nursing Homes Registration (Scotland) Act 1938 or a private hospital in respect of which registration is required under section 15 of the Mental Health (Scotland) Act 1960.
- Firearms dealer.
- Taxi driver.

Proof of entitlement to work

The Asylum and Immigration Act 1996 says that you have to get proof that people are entitled to work in this country before you can finally appoint them. Proof must consist of *either* one of the documents in List 1 *or* a combination of two documents as set out in List 2.

List 1 (one of these is sufficient)

- A passport showing that the person is a British Citizen, or has a right of abode in the UK.
- A document showing that the person is a national of a European Economic Area (EEA) country or Switzerland.
- A residence permit issued by the UK to a citizen from the EEA or Switzerland.
- A passport or other document issued by the Home Office which has an endorsement stating that the holder has a current right of residence in the UK as the family member of a national from the EEA or Switzerland.
- A passport or other document endorsed to show that the holder can stay indefinitely in the UK or has no time limit on their stay.
- A passport or other travel document endorsed to show that the holder can stay in the UK and that this endorsement allows the holder to do the type of work you are offering if they do not have a work permit.
- An Application Registration Card issued by the Home Office to an asylum seeker stating that the holder is permitted to take employment.

List 2 (you must see a specific combination of two documents)

Option A:

- A document giving the person's permanent National Insurance number and name. This could be a P45, P60, National Insurance card or a letter from a Government Agency.

and one of

- a full birth certificate issued in UK, which includes the names of the holder's parents;
- a birth certificate issued in Channel Islands, Isle of Man or Ireland;
- a certificate of registration or naturalisation stating that the holder is a British citizen;
- a letter issued by the Home Office which indicates that the person named in it can stay indefinitely in the UK or has no time limit on their stay can stay indefinitely or has no time limit on their stay;
- an Immigration Status Document issued by the Home Office with an endorsement indicating that the person named in it can stay indefinitely in the UK or has no time limit on their stay;
- a letter issued by the Home Office which indicates that the person named in it can stay in the UK; and this allows them to do the type of work you are offering;

- an Immigration Status Document issued by the Home Office with an endorsement indicating that the person named in it can stay in the UK; and this allows them to do the type of work you are offering.

Option B:

- a work permit or other approval to take employment that has been issued by Work Permits UK.

and one of

- a passport or other travel document endorsed to show that the holder is able to stay in the UK and can take the work permit employment in question;
- a letter issued by the Home Office confirming that the person named in it is able to stay in the UK and can take the work permit employment in question.

The wording given here is taken from a Home Office leaflet, but is not exactly the wording in the law.

Criminal Records Bureau checks

The Police Act 1997 introduced the Criminal Records Bureau (CRB) and makes it a requirement to check the criminal record of staff or volunteers working in specific posts in contact with children, while the Criminal Justice and Court Services Act 2000 sets out which types of post need CRB vetting before working with vulnerable adults.

For details of which posts should be checked at which level see www.crb.org.uk or www.disclosure.gov.uk.

There are three levels of check: Standard, Enhanced and Basic. Standard and enhanced disclosures are available only to employers who are registered with the CRB. Registration costs £300, plus £5 for each additional counter-signatory. This is a person able to sign applications on behalf of the registered body. Organisations which do not want to register themselves can get a check done through an umbrella body, if they can find one locally. These umbrella organisations may charge an administrative fee in addition to the charge for the check.

For a 'standard' disclosure the individual (employee or volunteer) and registered body apply jointly. The disclosure lists convictions which are 'spent' under the Rehabilitation of Offenders Act 1974, unspent convictions and cautions. For some types of work, an 'enhanced' disclosure is required, which lists in addition police information such as suspicions that did not lead to a caution or conviction.

From 1 April 2005 the fee is £29 for a standard disclosure and £34 for an enhanced disclosure, although for volunteers the fee is waived.

Any organisation registering with the CRB must comply with a code of practice, which requires organisations:

- to have a policy on the recruitment of ex-offenders;
- not to discriminate against candidates on the basis of unrelated offences;
- to handle disclosure information properly and in compliance with Data Protection Principles;
- to follow the CRB code of practice. Organisations must cooperate with checks by the CRB, and must report any suspected malpractice.

A registered umbrella body has to ensure that all organisations for which it handles CRB checks comply with the rules.

Eventually individuals will be able to obtain a basic disclosure, for use when they apply for jobs where a standard or enhanced disclosure is not required. This will cover only unspent convictions.

A separate disclosure service is operated by Disclosures Scotland (see the Resources section on page 00).

Establishments subject to the Care Standards Act

The Care Standards Act 2000 outlines what employment checks you must make on different categories of workers in different care settings, and what types of records must be held. The requirements can be found on the Commission for Care Standards Inspection web site. Separate regulations apply to a range of different types of organisation, and the web site (at January 2005) listed, among others, the following regulations, any of which might be relevant to voluntary organisations:

- The Care Homes Regulations 2001
- Children's Homes Regulations 2001
- Adult Placement Schemes Regulations 2004
- Domiciliary Care Regulations 2002
- Nurses Agencies Regulations 2002
- Residential Family Centres Regulations 2002
- Fostering Services Regulations 2002
- National Care Standards Commission (Registration) Regulations 2001
- Commission for Social Care Inspection (Fees and Frequency of Inspections) Regulations 2004
- Commission for Social Care Inspection (Children's Rights Director) Regulations 2004

- National Care Standards Commission (Inspections of Schools and Colleges) Regulations 2002
- The Care Standards Act 2000 (Establishments and Agencies) (Miscellaneous Amendments) Regulations 2002
- The Voluntary Adoption Agencies and the Adoption Agencies (Miscellaneous Amendment) Regulations 2003
- The National Care Standards Commission (Registration) (Amendment) Regulations 2003
- The National Care Standards Commission (Fees & Frequency of Inspections) (Adoption Agencies) Regulations 2003
- The Care Homes (Adult Placement) (Amendment) Regulations 2003
- The Care Standards Act 2000 (Establishments and Agencies) (Miscellaneous Amendments) Regulations 2004
- The Care Standards Act 2000 (Extension of the Application of Part 2 to Adult Placement Schemes) (England) Regulations 2004

Alongside the Regulations there is a set of National Minimum Standards for different types of establishment.

Separate inspection regimes operate, under specific legislation, in Scotland, Wales and Northern Ireland. See the Resources section (page 181).

Appendix B: Definitions of 'employee' and 'worker'

In law, 'employee' and 'worker' mean slightly different things, and carry with them different obligations in the workplace.

Confusingly, different bits of legislation have defined 'employee' differently. The Employment Right Act 1996 states that an employee is:

> *'An individual who has entered into or who works under (or, where the employment has ceased, worked under) a contract of employment.'*

But we also find:

> *'Employment means employment under a contract of service or apprenticeship or a contract personally to do any work.' (Disability Discrimination Act 1995)*

> *'Employment means employment under a contract of service or apprenticeship or a contract personally to execute any work or labour.' (Sex Discrimination Act and Race Relations Act)*

The definition of a 'worker' is wider. It is given in the Employment Rights Act 1996 (and also in the Working Time Regulations 1998 and the Part-time Workers Regulations 2000) as:

> *'An individual who has entered into or works under*
> *(a) a contract of employment; or*
> *(b) any other contract, whether express or implied and (if it is express) whether oral or in writing, whereby the individual undertakes to do or perform personally any work or services for another party to the contract whose status is not by virtue of the contract that of a client or customer of any profession or business undertaking carried out by the individual.'*

This means that an individual who operates as a business, such as an accountant or a computer engineer, is not a 'worker', even when they work for you in your office from time to time. A regular contractor who works mainly for one organisation might be a 'worker', while agency staff and home workers are almost certain to be 'workers' even if they are not employees.

Employees have different rights from workers who are not employees, and it is important for you to know which of your staff falls into which category when you are issuing them with documents and keeping records. Some of the most important provisions are given here.

Worker/employee rights	Employee	Worker
Maximum 48 hour week	Y	Y
Rest breaks	Y	Y
National minimum wage	Y	Y
SMP, SSP, SAP and SPP	Y	N
Protection from unfair dismissal (after 1 year's service)	Y	N
Redundancy rights (after 2 years' service)	Y	N
Minimum period of notice	Y	N
Right to be accompanied at a disciplinary or grievance hearing	Y	Y
Protection from discrimination (race, sex, disability, sexual orientation, religion or belief)	Y	Y (to contract workers)
Protection from discrimination (part-time workers)	Y	Y
Whistleblowing protection	Y	Y
Your responsibilities:		
CRB check those working with children or vulnerable adults	Y	Y
Have evidence of right to work in UK	Y	Y
Provide references (under Care Standards Act)	Y	Y

The Information Commissioner's Codes of Practice depart from the narrow definitions and use the term 'worker' to mean:

- applicants (successful and unsuccessful);
- former applicants (successful and unsuccessful);
- employees (current and former);
- agency staff (current and former);
- casual staff (current and former);
- contract staff (current and former).

This wide definition only applies in this specific context. Former employees, for example, are not workers in relation to their employment rights, but they may still be Data Subjects under the Data Protection Act, and therefore their records need to be handled according to the same principles as those of current employees. We have retained the term 'worker' in the extracts from the Commissioner's Code; elsewhere we generally prefer the term 'staff' or 'personnel' as a non-specific way of referring to people who work for an organisation in the full range of possible relationships.

Appendix C: Sample subject access request form

Date received:

[NAME OF ORGANISATION]

Subject Access request form for paid staff and volunteers

You are entitled under the 1998 Data Protection Act to see most of the information we hold about you. We also operate an open files policy, which allows you to see much of the same information informally. If you are not sure which option is best for you, please discuss it with the personnel department before completing this form.

Your name:

The department/location where you work:

Are we likely to have any information about you other than personnel records? (For example are you also a member of the organisation?) If so, please tell us here:

If you are interested only in part of the information we hold, please explain what in particular you want to see:

When we have located the information about you, do you want to:

☐   have a look at it at the personnel department
☐   collect a copy from the personnel department
☐   have us send a copy to your home address

I want access to the records you hold on me, and I enclose the fee of £10.

Signature:

Please note:

■   If you are making this application on behalf of someone else, we will need to see evidence that you have been authorised to do so.
■   We will reply as quickly as we can. We aim to reply within two weeks, but we may legally take up to 40 days.
■   We will show you everything we have about you, except that we may be allowed to hold back or provide edited versions of certain information, especially if it is from, or about, someone else. This may include confidential references we have been given or have provided to other people.

Appendix D: Application form template

The form is structured as follows.

Page 1 and back of page 1 (detachable from the rest of the form)	Personal information, referees, equal opportunities monitoring
Page 2	Work history
Pages 3 and 4	Meeting the person specification criteria
Page 5	Education and training Declarations of unspent convictions and of giving truthful information

The sample form that occupies the next five pages is for the same post as that in the shortlisting form in Appendix F — a job that does not require a CRB check and is not exempt under the Rehabilitation of Offenders Act 1974.

Following the sample form are additional or alternative sections and pages which might apply in a variety of other circumstances.

In order to make use of the material, you would obviously have to prepare a version specific to your organisation, probably with your logo, address and other details, in addition to adapting the sample here to your exact situation.

[Page 1]

Personal details

Post applied for:

Surname/Family name:

Address:

Phone number at work (if we may contact you there):

Phone number at home:

Our Ref:

Reference No. of post:

First name(s):

Referees

References are normally taken up only if we want to offer you the post. If we want to contact referees earlier than that, we will only do this with your permission.

Please give details of two people who can comment on your suitability for this job. Wherever possible they should be your current and most recent previous employers. Other examples might be a college tutor, community leader or someone in a position of responsibility (for example in an organisation where you did voluntary work).

	Referee 1	Referee 2
Referee name:		
How they know you:		
Organisation they work for:		
Referee's job title:		
Referee's address:		
Referee's phone number:		

[Back of page 1]

Equal opportunities monitoring form

We hope you will assist us by filling in this monitoring form. This information is being gathered to monitor our recruitment procedure, and the effectiveness of advertising media and for no other purpose. The data will not be taken into account in shortlisting, because it is detached form the form before the panel see it. If you prefer not to answer any question this will not affect your application.

Are you   ☐ Male   ☐ Female

(The following ethnic origin categories have been selected to reflect the Commission for Racial Equality and the Department of Health's recommendations.)

What is your ethnic group?

a) White
☐ British
☐ Irish
☐ Any other white background
(Please write in below)

b) Mixed
☐ White and Black Caribbean
☐ White and Black African
☐ White and Asian
☐ Any other mixed background
(Please write in below)

c) Asian or Asian British
☐ Indian
☐ Pakistani
☐ Bangladeshi
☐ Any other Asian background
(Please write in below)

d) Black or Black British
☐ Caribbean
☐ African
☐ Any other Black background *(Please write in below)*

e) Chinese or other ethnic group
☐ Chinese
☐ Any other group *(Please write in below)*

Marital status: Are you   ☐ Married   ☐ Single   ☐ Other

Disability: Disability is defined as a physical or mental impairment, which has a substantial and long-term effect on a person's ability to carry out their day-to-day activities.
     In these terms, do you consider you have a disability   ☐ Yes ☐ No

Are you applying under the Guaranteed Interview Scheme (GIS)   ☐ Yes ☐ No
See details at the end of the application form.

How did you hear about this vacancy?
         ☐   Advert (which paper/journal)
         ☐   Job Centre

[Page 2]   Our Ref:

Details of last or current employment

Name and address of employer:

Dates employed   From: To:

Reason for leaving:

Notice required (if currently in post):

Briefly describe your current/most recent employment, highlighting duties, responsibilities, skills or experience gained that are relevant to the post you are applying for.

Details of previous employment

(including home-based, voluntary or part-time work)

Please provide details of your employment history to date, starting with your most recent. Please account for any periods of time spent in further education or employment.

Name/address of employer	Position Held and grade	From (mm/yy)	To (mm/yy)	Reason for leaving

Our Ref:

Your ability to meet the essential criteria for the post

The job description for this post details the key areas of responsibility and outcomes of this post. The person specification sets out key areas of skills and abilities, knowledge, education, training and qualifications that are essential for the post-holder to have. Please demonstrate in this section how you meet the person specification requirements.

Shortlisting will depend on how well you demonstrate your ability to meet the criteria. Do not just assert that you can do something, give us evidence of experience or how you know it. Include relevant voluntary or non-work experience as well as experience from previous employment. You may add a continuation page if necessary.

Experience of office administration, reception and teamwork

Ability to communicate with a wide range of people

Writing and word processing skills

Working with and motivating volunteers

[Page 4]   Our Ref:

Your ability to meet the essential criteria for the post (continued)

Use of office equipment

What do you understand by equal opportunities?

Knowledge of health and safety

What do you understand by confidentiality?

Our Ref:

Education/Training/Qualifications

Please list any training courses undertaken and or qualifications obtained which you consider to be relevant to the post.

Course   Qualification Body   Dates   Grade (if applicable)

Relevant unspent convictions

A previous conviction will not necessarily bar you from getting this job, but you must tell us here of any unspent convictions you have. This information will not be disclosed to anyone except the shortlisting and interview panel.

Declaration

I declare that the information on this form is true and correct to the best of my knowledge. I understand that if it is subsequently discovered that any statement is false or misleading, my employment may be ended without notice.

I consent to my referees disclosing information about my attendance and sickness record.

Signed .... Date ....

[If you are signed up to the Disability Symbol the following material may also be relevant.]

Guaranteed Interview Scheme

We are committed to the employment and career development of disabled people. To demonstrate our commitment we are working towards the Disability Symbol which is awarded by the Employment Service. We guaranteed an interview to anyone with a disability whose application meets the minimum criteria for the post.

What do we mean by disability?

To be eligible for the scheme you must meet the definition of disabled under the Disability Discrimination Act. You must have a long-term disability or health condition which puts you at a disadvantage in either obtaining or keeping jobs. The disability could be physical, sensory or mental and must have lasted or be expected to last at least 12 months.

How do I apply?

Complete the declaration below and let us know if there is any help you need in completing the form or if you would like it in an alternative format please contact the Personnel Department on Telephone number...........

Declaration

I consider myself to have a disability as defined above and I would like to apply under the Guaranteed Interview Scheme.

Name .... Date ....

Signed ....

[Additional material relevant where CRB checks are required and/or the post is not exempt under the Rehabilitation of Offenders Act 1974, to replace the section on convictions in the sample above.]

Declaration of offences

This position is exempt from the provisions of the Rehabilitation of Offenders Act 1974. Applicants are therefore required to declare all convictions (including traffic offences and juvenile convictions) which are for other purposes 'spent' under the Act. We aim to provide equality of opportunity for all applicants including those with a criminal record. Criminal convictions will only be taken into account where they are relevant.

This post is required to have a Standard Criminal Records Bureau disclosure.

Do you have any spent or unspent convictions, cautions, reprimands or final warnings from the police to disclose? ☐ Yes ☐ No

If the answer is 'Yes', please give details of all offences, penalties and dates here:

I confirm that this information is correct and complete. I understand that because of the nature of the post, my declaration must include all the details specified above. I understand too that a Criminal Records Bureau disclosure will be required in the event of my application being successful.

Signed .... Date ....

[For Enhanced disclosures, replace the relevant sections above with the following.]

This post is required to have an Enhanced Criminal Records Bureau disclosure.

Do you have any spent or unspent convictions, cautions, reprimands or final warnings from the police or any other information such as police enquiries undertaken following allegations made against you to disclose? ☐ Yes ☐ No

If the answer is 'Yes', please give details of all offences, penalties and dates here:

[For posts subject to either Standard or Enhanced CRB checks, replace the statement on referees with the following.]

Please give a minimum of two referees, who can cover the last five years of your employment. The first referee must be: your current employer and your relevant line manager if you are employed; your last employer if you are unemployed; your head teacher or college tutor if this is your first job. You may also provide the name of a personal referee.

[The following is sometimes included on an application form, although it would probably be more appropriate to accompany a letter inviting the appplicant for interview.]

Assistance for interview

Please let us know if you would like any particular assistance for your interview, such as (please tick):

☐ Induction loop

☐ Sign language interpreter (please say what type)

☐ Keyboard for written tests

☐ Someone with you at interview (speech facilitator)

☐ Car parking

☐ Assistance in and out of a vehicle

☐ Wheelchair access

☐ Accessible toilet facilities

☐ Other assistance (please specify)

If you have any queries about your specific needs at the interview or would like to give us more information please contact the Personnel Department.

Appendix E: Sample reference request letter

Dear *[name]*

Reference for *[name]* of *[address]*

I am writing to request a written reference for *[name]*, who has been selected (pending successful references) for the post of *[job title]* (job description enclosed) at *[organisation's name]* and has given your name as a referee.

Could you confirm that they have been working for you as [.......] since [.....].

I would like you to provide a detailed reference as to how well in your view or experience they meet the criteria on the person specification included with this letter. Could you cover each criterion separately please? If you feel you cannot comment on any point, please say why, briefly.

I would also like to know how many days sick leave *[name]* has taken over the last year, and whether they were spread out or consecutive. The applicant has given consent to your disclosure of this information.

If you would like to clarify any of these points please telephone me at the above number, but please note that we are unable to accept a telephone reference.

I would be obliged if you could give this a high priority as we cannot make the appointment until all references have been received.

Once you have given us the reference, and if the person is appointed, the reference will be stored on their personnel file and they will be able to see it unless you specify that you would prefer it to be confidential. We will assume that you are happy for the reference you provide to be seen by the individual concerned should they get the job, unless you give reasons why you consider all or part of it should remain confidential.

I enclose a stamped addressed envelope for your reply, which will be held in strictest confidence to the selection panel.

Yours sincerely

Chair of the selection panel

Encs
Job description
Person Specification

Appendix F: Sample shortlisting form

SHORTLISTING FORM: Office Administrator		Fully met	Partly met	Not met
Experience	One year (paid) in office administration			
	Ordering stationery, dealing with office suppliers and maintenance contracts			
	Reception duties including operating a switchboard			
	Working supportively in a team environment			
Skills and abilities	Ability to communicate clearly and assertively with a wide range of people			
	Clear written style in minute taking			
	Word processing skills to 50 wpm			
	Working constructively with and motivating volunteers			
Knowledge	Manual and computerised office administration systems such as (specify....)			
	The use of a range of office equipment			
	Equal opportunity policies and practices			
	Health and safety issues affecting staff and volunteers and willingness to be trained in risk assessments if not already qualified			
	Clear understanding of confidentiality in written and computerised materials and processes			
Education/ Training	GCSE English and Maths or equivalent			
Other	Based at London Head Office			
	Willing to travel to annual staff conference and stay overnight			

Appendix G: Sample letter of appointment

Dear *[name]*

I am happy to confirm your appointment as *[job title]* on *[hours]* at an annual salary/hourly rate of *[amount]* subject to receipt of satisfactory references and vetting from the Criminal Records Bureau (Standard or Enhanced Check) and confirmation of your right to work in the UK.

We would like you to start with us on *[start date]* at *[start time]*. On that day please report to reception at *[place of work]* and ask for *[name]*.

You should bring your P45 (or your National Insurance number). In order for me to ensure that you receive your pay on time, please complete the enclosed form about your bank details and return to me. Your first payment will be made on *[date]*.

Enclosed you will find two copies of a statement of your terms and conditions of employment, a notice about personal information and a copy of the staff handbook. These documents contain important information about your terms of employment so please read them carefully.

Please confirm that you accept these terms of employment by signing one copy of the statement and personal information notice and returning them to me as soon as possible. The other copy of the statement and personal information notice and the Handbook are for you to keep, for your own reference.

Once you have begun work you will be taken through an induction programme, during which our policies and procedures will be explained to you and you will have an opportunity to ask any questions that you may have about your conditions of employment.

Because of the Working Time Directive, we need to ensure that you do not work more than 48 hours a week in total. If you have any job other than this one, you must inform Personnel on your first day.

Please note that the first six months of your employment will be treated as a probationary period, during which time your performance will be monitored to ensure that you are suitable for the job. If your performance proves to be unsatisfactory, your employment may be terminated during or at the end of your probationary period.

May I take this opportunity to welcome you to the organisation, and to wish you every success in your career with us.

Signed ....   Date ....

Appendix H: Sample letters related to varying the contract

Dear *[name]*

The organisation has recently reviewed the written statement of terms and conditions of employment (your contract of employment). We have sought expert advice in order to ensure that our terms and conditions are fully up-to-date and comply with good practice.

The revised contract which is enclosed is mainly a tidying up exercise but does include a number of improvements for employees, including:
[........................]

There is only one reduction in the terms and conditions, which is [........................]

We will be consulting with staff for a period of one month from [...............] and if you have any concerns please feel free to raise them with the Personnel Office. We will also be organising staff briefings when you will have the opportunity to discuss any concerns.

Once the briefings and consultation have taken place we will consider any points raised and then issue a final contract for signing.

Yours sincerely

Dear *[name]*

As you know we have carried out a consultation exercise concerning the terms and conditions of employment. This consultation has now ended and enclosed are two copies of the new terms and conditions.

Please sign both copies and return one copy to this office. If you do not wish to sign for any reason please see the Personnel Office as soon as possible to discuss this matter.

Yours sincerely

Appendix I: Sample induction programme record sheet

Name of staff member:.............	Induction supervisor:		
Activity	Person responsible	Date complete	Initials of staff member
Introduction			
Introduction to organisation			
Structure of the organisation			
Tour of building and introductions			
Fire and emergency arrangements			
Training in security procedures			
Entry pass issued			
Review of contract terms			
Policies issued (e.g. confidentiality)			
Policies signed and returned			
Staff handbook issued			
Details to personnel department			
Details to finance department			
Toilets and refreshments			
Parking/Cycling arrangements			
Photocopiers and stationery supplies			
Set up computer network account			
Computer induction (including AUP)			
The work			
Their office space			
Meeting the team or department			
Work plan			
Team meetings			
Supervision arrangements			
Induction review (after one week)			
Training necessary to the job completed			

Name of staff member:.............	Induction supervisor:		
Activity	Person responsible	Date complete	Initials of staff member
Further training requirements discussed			
Background reading issued			
Who's who			
Meeting with ...			
Meeting with ...			
Meeting with ...			
Meeting with ...			

Appendix J: Sample forms recording holidays, sickness absence, maternity absence and time off

Pre-arranged leave

Details will be held in strict confidence

Full Name:

Department:

First day of proposed leave: Last day of proposed leave:

Date of return to work:

Total time of leave: days   hours

Reason: Holiday ☐ TOIL ☐ Public duties ☐ Medical/Dental appointment ☐

Other reason:

How many days has this employee already taken for this reason in this holiday year?

Is the proposed leave: Paid ☐   Unpaid ☐

I request authorised leave as described above: .... (signed) .... (date)

....

Leave request considered by: .... (name of manager) on .... (date)

Leave authorised: .... (signed)

Leave not authorised for the following reason:

.... (signed)

....

If the requested leave is not authorised, the manager must give a copy of this form to the employee, who can then appeal the decision.

It will be assumed that the leave takes place as shown on this form. If there are any variations, it is the responsibility of the employee to ensure that the personnel department is informed.

Absence/lateness report where not pre-arranged

Details will be held in strict confidence

Full Name:

Department:

First day of absence: Last day of proposed absence:

Date of return to work: Total time of leave: days   hours

Reason: Sick ☐   Domestic or child care emergency ☐

Other reason:

When did you notify the organisation of your absence?

Whom did you notify?

Complete the following if your absence was due to sickness

Did you consult your doctor?   Yes ☐   No ☐

If YES please give the date of the appointment:

Name of doctor: Phone number:

Address of doctor:

Did you obtain a medical certificate? (Please attach where applicable)

                                                                Yes ☐   No ☐

Are you taking any medication?   Yes ☐   No ☐ If YES, please give details:

If YES, have you advised of any side effects which could affect your work or be a safety hazard?   Yes ☐   No ☐

Do you consider that your work in any way contributed to your ill health?
Yes ☐   No ☐   If YES, please give details:

[continued]

DECLARATION

I declare that all the information I have given in this form is true and that I have not withheld any material fact.

I understand these details will be held in confidence by the organisation and may be used for the following purposes:

- ensuring the health, safety and welfare at work of myself and other workers;
- the avoidance of discrimination on the grounds of disability;
- maintaining Statutory Sick Pay and Statutory Maternity Pay records;
- supplying information on accidents where industrial injury benefits may be payable;
- ensuring the organisation is able to monitor and deal fairly with attendance and absence issues.

Signature of employee: .... Date: ....

Absence report considered by: .... (name of manager) on .... (date)

Absence authorised: ....(signed)

Please note that by authorising the absence you are confirming that you are satisfied that the employee had a valid reason for being absent and that the employee has complied with all notification and certification procedures.

Absence not authorised for the following reason:

.... (signed)

If the reason for the absence is not authorised, the manager must give a copy of this form to the employee, who can then appeal the decision.

Time off and sickness absence record card

EMPLOYEE'S NAME:

YEAR:

	1	2	3	4	5	6	7	8	9	10	11	12	13	14	15	16	17	18	19	20	21	22	23	24	25	26	27	28	29	30	31
JAN																															
FEB																															
MAR																															
APR																															
MAY																															
JUN																															
JUL																															
AUG																															
SEP																															
OCT																															
NOV																															
DEC																															

YEAR:

	1	2	3	4	5	6	7	8	9	10	11	12	13	14	15	16	17	18	19	20	21	22	23	24	25	26	27	28	29	30	31
JAN																															
FEB																															
MAR																															
APR																															
MAY																															
JUN																															
JUL																															
AUG																															
SEP																															
OCT																															
NOV																															
DEC																															

Use these codes to indicate the reason for absence:

H	Holiday	J	Jury service	AD	Adoption
S	Sick	P	Public duties	AN	Ante Natal
T	Time off in lieu	SL	Study leave	M	Maternity
U	Unauthorised absence	TU	Trade union duties	PL	Parental
A	Other authorised absence	PT	Paternity		
L	Late (followed by number of minutes)*				

* Optional: see Chapter 12

[This form is illustrative only. You must check the most up to date legal position and your contractual provision before drawing up a form for your own use.]

Maternity absence record

Name of employee:		
Date pregnancy notified:		(In writing if employer requests [recommended])
Monday of expected week of childbirth:		(Medical evidence required, if SMP to be claimed)
Date employment started:		(In order to calculate whether additional maternity leave is due)
Additional maternity leave due?	Calculated automatically	(Yes or no)
Date by which employee must state intention to take maternity leave:	Calculated automatically	(By 15th week before expected week of childbirth)
Earliest date maternity leave can start:	Calculated automatically	(Start of 11th week before expected week of childbirth)
Date employee wishes to start maternity leave:		(Employee must give 28 days' notice of any change of date)
Expected date of return:	Calculated automatically	(Either 26 weeks after start date, or 52 weeks if Additional Leave is due)
Date employee notified of expected date of return:		(Response must be given within 28 days of employee's notification)
Actual start date of maternity leave:		(May be earlier than notified date in cases of illness or early birth)
Actual date maternity leave is due to end:	Calculated automatically	(Either 26 weeks after start date, or 52 weeks if Additional Maternity Leave is due)
Date employee notifies intention to return to work before end of leave:		(Need not be in writing; not required if returning at end of entitlement)
Earliest date employee may return early:	Calculated automatically	(Must be at least 28 days after notice given)

Appendix K: Statutory rights to time off

	Amount	Length of service to qualify	With pay?	How much pay?	Who is eligible?
Family/Dependent's leave					
Ordinary maternity leave	26 weeks	None	See SMP	See SMP	Pregnant employees
Additional maternity leave	A further 26 weeks	Entitled to ordinary maternity leave	No		Pregnant employees
Time off for ante natal care	Enough to keep her appointment	None	Yes	Normal	Pregnant employees
Statutory Maternity Pay (SMP)		26 weeks at end of 15th week prior to expected week of childbirth	Yes	90% of full salary for 6 weeks and 20 weeks on SMP or 90% of weekly earnings if lower	Pregnant employees
Paternity leave	Up to 2 weeks	26 weeks at end of 15th week prior to expected week of childbirth or week in which the adopter is notified of match	Yes	Statutory Paternity Pay at lesser of SPP rate or 90% of average earnings	Employees who are fathers and other partners on the birth or adoption of a child - must meet eligibility criteria
Ordinary adoption leave	26 weeks	26 weeks at end of 15th week in which the adopter is notified of match	Yes	Statutory Adoption Pay see SPP above	Employees who must be the child's adopter
Additional adoption leave	A further 26 weeks	If took SAL and it did not end prematurely	No		Employees who must be the child's adopter
Parental leave	13 weeks (18 weeks if child is disabled) max 4 weeks in any 1 year	1 year and expect to have responsibility for a child. If change jobs have to qualify again	No		Both parents of young or recently adopted children up to age 5 (18 if disabled) and meet eligibility requirements
Dependent's leave	Reasonable	None	No		Short term emergency for spouse, child or parent, someone living with you (not lodger or tenant or employee) or someone who relies on you for care
Holidays and sickness					
Holidays	4 weeks in one year	Pro rata entitlement in 1st year	Yes	Normal	Employees and Workers
Sickness	Payable for 28 weeks	None. Have to be ill and have to meet certification requirements	Yes	SSP	Employees

	Amount	Length of service to qualify	With pay?	How much pay?	Who is eligible?
Rights for trade unionists and employees' reps					
Trade union officials and learning reps	Reasonable time to take part in trade union duties	None	Yes	Normal	Shop stewards, branch officers and officials of the recognised union
Trade union members	Reasonable time to take part in trade union activities	None	No	By negotiation or contract	Members of recognised union
Safety reps (union)	As necessary for training and duties	None	Yes	Normal	Reps appointed by recognised union with collective bargaining and negotiation rights
Safety reps (no union)	As necessary for training, duties and election	None	Yes	Normal	Reps elected by workforce where no recognised union
Employees' reps handling redundancies and TUPE	Reasonable	None	Yes	Normal	Reps elected by workforce where no recognised union
Pension scheme trustees	Reasonable	None	Yes	Normal	Trustees of occupational pensions schemes
Other time off					
Public duties	Reasonable	None	Need not be paid	If it is paid by negotiation or contract	Summarised as: JP, councillor; member of: a tribunal; a police authority; the NCIS authority; a board of prison visitors; health, education or water authority[1]
When redundant, to seek work	Reasonable	2 years' service	Yes	40% of a week's pay during redundancy notice period	Employees under notice of redundancy
Time off for study or training	For training	None	Yes	Normal	16 and17 year olds who left school without a prescribed level of qualification. An 18 year old who started a course under these provisions can finish it – ends at age 19
Accompany a worker to a disciplinary or grievance hearing	To go to the hearing	None	Yes	Normal	Trade union official or workplace colleague

[1]See s50 of Employment rights Act 1996.

Appendix L: Sample supervision record form

Supervision meeting agenda and record

....

1. Review agenda
2. Practical matters – TOIL/Holidays/Sickness, other contract or terms issues
3. Health and safety and issues of risk
4. Review of individual performance and objectives from last time
5. Discussion of new issues
6. Feedback to the manager on support provided and ideas/suggestions
7. Team issues
8. Training needs
9. Objectives for next session

....

Staff member: Manager:

Date held:

1   Any additional agenda items (including issues to be raised under item 4)?

2   Practical matters – TOIL/Holidays/Sickness/Other matters/Health & Safety concerns?

Issue/Question   How to address   Action

3   Review of last time's objectives

OBJECTIVE	OUTCOME	LEARNING/FURTHER ACTION?

4   Discussion of new performance issues

Issue/Question   How to address   Action

5   Feedback to the manager on support provided and ideas/suggestions

6   Team or organisational issues affecting the employee

Issue/Question   How to address   Action

7   Training needs

Training need   How to address   Action

8   Objectives for next session.

Signed ....   Date ....
             Manager
Signed ....   Date ....
             Employee

Appendix M: Sample staff handbook contents list

[Based on the staff handbook of a large national care organisation.]

1 Joining the organisation

1.1 Induction

1.2 Probation

1.3 Respect for others

1.4 Reporting abuse of residents/clients

1.5 Reporting criminal convictions

2 During employment

2.1 Place of work

2.2 Tips, gifts and loans

2.3 Confidentiality

2.4 Residents'/clients' records

2.5 Use of computers, emails and internet access

2.6 Personal calls and mobiles

2.7 Radios and stereos

2.8 Smoking

2.9 Appearance

2.10 Personal property

2.11 Employee suggestions

2.12 Information we keep on you

2.13 Change in personal details

3 Communications and staff relations

3.1 Staff meetings

3.2 Staff code of conduct

8 Sickness absence policy and procedures

8.1 Introduction

8.2 Probation

8.3 Processing of information

8.4 Summary of responsibilities

8.5 Procedures for reporting absence for employee

8.6 Sickness certificates

8.7 Entitlements

8.8 Sickness and annual leave

8.9 Failure to follow absence recording procedures

8.10 Returning to work

8.11 Visits

9 Other leave

9.1 Compassionate leave

9.2 Leave for education and development

9.3 Medical appointments

9.4 Unpaid Leave

9.5 Extended leave

9.6 Public duties

10 Staff supervision, training and development

10.1 Supervision

10.2 Appraisal

10.3 Training and development

Appendix N: Sample IT and internet acceptable use policy

Introduction

E-mail and web access are made available for communication on matters directly concerned with the activities of the organisation. The organisation recognises that they are valuable tools, but that their misuse can expose the organisation and its staff to risks. Inappropriate use can result in:

- damage to relationships with colleagues, service users, members, suppliers and the general public;
- legal consequences for the organisation, for example over a contract unintentionally created using e-mail;
- bullying, harassment or discrimination, for which the organisation as well as individual staff may be liable;
- failure of the organisation to comply with its legal responsibilities;
- information overload when information is sent to people who do not need it;
- diversion of staff away from their official duties;
- additional cost to the organisation.

This policy therefore applies to all staff (including volunteers) who are provided with IT facilities, whether at an office of the organisation or from home. The policy will be monitored, and breach of the policy will result in disciplinary action. Some breaches will count as gross misconduct.

The term 'internet' is used to encompass e-mail, the world wide web and other services such as instant messaging or chat forums.

Use of IT and communications facilities

The organisation's equipment is provided to benefit the organisation's work. However, employees are permitted *reasonable* use of the internet and telephone in their own time for private purposes, provided that such use is not detrimental to their job responsibilities.

'Reasonable' means occasional, and for short periods, for example using the telephone to arrange a doctor's appointment or tell family that you are working late. Use of the web for lengthy periods – even during lunch and other breaks – is not permitted. Lengthy personal phone calls may not be made or received, except in exceptional circumstances.

Employees must only use licensed software and must not download or install any software without the permission of the IT Manager. This applies even if a web site offers to download and/or install software in order to provide facilities that are needed for work-related purposes.

Employees are not permitted to remain in the office after normal working hours in order to use the telephone, internet or IT system for private purposes.

Employees are not permitted to store personal address lists or other personal data on the organisation's systems, other than in the course of limited internet use.

Action will be taken in the case of excessive use of the organisation's facilities, or any use that is detrimental to work performance.

Unacceptable use

The organisation will not tolerate the use of the IT system for any of the following.

- Any e-mail or web posting that could constitute bullying or harassment on the grounds of gender, race, religion, disability, sexuality or age, any defamatory or fraudulent statement, or any activity that is illegal. (*)
- Access to any pornographic, racist or otherwise offensive material, or to web sites which clearly offer such material. (*) Any employee receiving or accessing such material inadvertently must immediately inform the IT Manager, and must co-operate fully in any measures necessary to expunge the material.
- Participation in chat rooms, unless these are specifically work related and the employee has the express permission of their line manager.
- Playing internet games or online gambling. (*)
- Use of the organisation's facilities for the personal profit of the employee. (*) Employees should not normally make private financial transactions of any kind over the internet.
- Downloading or distributing copyright information without authorisation.
- Personal use for sending social invitations, trivial personal messages, jokes, cartoons, chain letters or large attachments of any kind. Receipt of any such material is discouraged, and employees are expected to inform regular correspondents not to send such material to them at work.
- Deliberately subverting the virus checker or any other security measure, whether on the organisation's equipment or anyone else's. (*)
- Disclosure of a work e-mail address on any web site not related to work, such that unsolicited e-mail (spam) might be attracted.
- Sending e-mails or other messages in another person's name or accessing another person's e-mail without their explicit consent. (*)
- Misrepresentation of personal views or interests as being those of the organisation.

Those activities followed by (*) will normally be treated as gross misconduct.

E-mail content

In addition to the provisions above, employees must ensure that the content of all e-mails sent using the organisation's system is appropriate, to avoid embarrassment or adverse legal consequences to the organisation or the employee. E-mails must avoid giving offence, and must not conflict with any policy of the organisation.

Employees must not under any circumstances send defamatory or intemperately critical material about individuals or other organisations, even internally to colleagues. It is inadvisable to send e-mails when angry, as there is little opportunity to review the content or to retrieve a message sent inappropriately.

E-mails carry the same weight as any other written document, and agreements or contracts made by e-mail are legally binding. Employees must not place orders or enter into agreements by e-mail unless they are authorised to do so. Where there is no intention to enter into a contract, the e-mail must make this explicit.

The style and content of an e-mail message must be consistent with the standards that the organisation expects from any other written communication. Guidelines include the following.

- Use informative subject lines, to ensure that the recipient can identify the relevance of your message to them.
- Always identify yourself and put the name of the organisation, your full name, job title and direct phone contact at the end of an e-mail.
- Ensure that any information, including the company number and charity number, which is on the headed paper also appears on e-mails to new contacts, or with a wide circulation.
- Take time to check for clarity, grammar and spelling. Remember that humour does not always come over as intended in an e-mail; avoid it unless you are very sure that it will be appreciated.
- Do not use unfamiliar abbreviations or UPPERCASE. Individual words may be emphasised by enclosing them in *asterisks* rather than bold or italics.
- When forwarding e-mails do not change any of the original text, and make it clear which part is the original and which is your additional comments.
- Always add the agreed disclaimer at the end of each e-mail.

E-mail recipients may not have high-speed communications links; they may also be affected by information overload. It is discourteous to impose on anyone an unnecessary burden of time or cost. For this reason:

- send e-mails as plain text rather than HTML or other formats;
- do not send attachments of more than 500Kb without checking that this is acceptable to the recipient;

- do not routinely use the organisation's logo or other graphical material in e-mails, unless these are essential to the content;
- send messages only to those to whom they are relevant. Do not copy or forward messages unless you are sure it is necessary. Do not over-use large mailing lists or groups of recipients.

E-mail should not be used as a substitute for face-to-face communication, or to avoid difficult or potentially unpleasant conversations, especially within the building. For external communications a telephone call may be more appropriate.

Any outgoing personal e-mails must be marked as 'personal' and incoming ones must be stored in a 'personal' e-mail folder. Otherwise they will be treated as being related to the organisation.

Confidentiality, security and data protection

E-mail is not necessarily less secure than other forms of communication, but care must still be taken to preserve confidentiality and to avoid disclosing information in any way that will cause harm or inconvenience.

Any disclosure of information about individuals must be within the terms of the organisation's Data Protection Policy.

Confidential information should not be sent by e-mail without good reason. Where possible it should be protected, for example by putting the confidential material in an attached document which has a password.

Before sending confidential information, the sender must be absolutely certain that the address it is being sent to is correct and appropriate.

When replying to an e-mail all information should be deleted that the reply does not need to contain, especially if the reply is being copied to other people.

Recipients' e-mail addresses must not be disclosed to other people unnecessarily. For a message going to several people who do not (or may not) already know each other's addresses, the BCC: field or a mailing list should be used, instead of putting all the recipients' addresses in the To: or CC: field.

Personal system passwords must not be disclosed to other staff, volunteers or external users unless sanctioned by the IT Manager.

Important data must be kept on the appropriate network drive. Any information on the local C: drive will not be centrally backed up.

Although the organisation has virus protection in place, all employees are also expected to take suitable precautions against viruses and other unwanted material.

This means:

- not having the preview window open;
- deleting – without opening – any e-mail that gives any cause for concern in its source or subject line;
- not opening any attachment unless there is reason to believe that it is genuine;
- reporting any virus warning to the IT Manager before taking any action or passing the warning on to anyone at all. Most virus 'warnings' are hoaxes.

Monitoring

As far as possible the organisation will use automated systems to block access to inappropriate web sites or to filter out unacceptable e-mails, in order to avoid breaching employees' privacy.

Employees should be aware that no e-mail sent or received using the organisation's systems, and no web session, can be considered totally private. All activity on the system, including deleted files, leaves an audit trail and may potentially be recovered.

The organisation will routinely monitor e-mail traffic and web sites accessed, at random across the organisation.

Where there is apparent excessive use of the internet for personal reasons, access to inappropriate web sites or any other apparent breach of this policy, the organisation reserves the right to investigate further. This investigation may involve more detailed monitoring of the content of the employee's internet use, including material identified as personal if this is appropriate in all the circumstances. The IT Manager will carry out such investigation only with authorisation from a member of the Senior Management Team, who must be satisfied that the case for investigation has been made, and that the type of investigation being proposed is proportionate to the apparent breach of policy.

Employees will normally be informed that they are being investigated or monitored. In exceptional cases covert monitoring will be authorised where it is the only reasonable way of obtaining evidence of criminal activity or continuing gross misconduct, and it is necessary to avoid alerting the employee.

E-mails and files held under an employee's name on the organisation's IT system may be accessed when an employee is away from the office if it is necessary for the business of the organisation. This action will only be taken by the IT Manager at the request of the absent employee's line manager, and where the absence is either unplanned or likely to be lengthy, or in an emergency.

When access is obtained for this purpose, care will be taken not to open or read any e-mail or other file which is clearly personal.

Wherever possible, employees planning to be absent should make their own arrangements for work-related e-mails and files to be accessible to colleagues.

Complaints

Any employee being harassed or with cause for complaint in how the e-mail system is being used, should contact their Head of Department immediately.

Consent

I have read the above policy on use of e-mail and internet and I agree to the monitoring described.

Signed ....

Name ....

Date ....

Appendix O: Sample leaver's checklist

Name of staff member: Last day of work: Reason for leaving:	Date complete	Initials of responsible staff member
Before departure		
Notice of intention to leave received in writing or dismissal notice issued		
Holiday owing/taken in advance agreed		
Plan made for outstanding TOIL to be taken		
Outstanding loan(s) recovered		
List prepared of property to be returned		
Handing-over notes for successor prepared		
Consulted on job description of replacement, if appropriate		
Induction of successor planned, if possible		
Check forwarding address		
At or around departure		
P45 prepared and given to employee		
Keys, security cards handed in		
Equipment and clothing belonging to employer handed back		
Final briefing for successor/stand-in on outstanding tasks		
Exit interview carried out		
Agree scope of future references to be provided		
Replace employee as contact for mailings, representative on working parties, etc.		
Pay final salary, making necessary adjustments		
After departure (as soon as possible)		
Authorities notified, if required by dismissal for misconduct		
Computer access cancelled, passwords reset		
Security access cancelled		
Internal telephone directory updated		
Suppliers/service contractors notified that individual is no longer authorised to purchase on behalf of organisation		
Line managers' records of supervisions, etc, returned to personnel department		